Cyber Election Meddling: The Impact on Voter Beliefs and Decisions

Dr. Faton Aliu

BookLocker

Trenton, Georgia

Print ISBN: 978-1-959621-57-7
Ebook ISBN: 979-8-88531-878-5

Published by BookLocker.com, Inc., Trenton, Georgia.

BookLocker.com, Inc.
2024

First Edition

Library of Congress Cataloging in Publication Data
Aliu, Dr. Faton
Cyber Election Meddling: The Impact on Voter Beliefs and Decisions by Dr. Faton Aliu
Library of Congress Control Number: 2024923106

Voters' Belief in Cyber Election Meddling and its Impact on
their Decision-making Process in Government Elections

Dissertation Manuscript

Submitted to Ecole des Ponts
Business School

in Partial Fulfillment of the
Requirements for the Degree of
DOCTOR OF BUSINESS ADMINISTRATION

by

Faton Aliu
Paris, France

May 2024

DISCLAIMER

This book details the author's personal research and opinions regarding cyber-election meddling and its impact on voter beliefs and decision-making. The author is not a licensed political scientist or attorney.

The author and publisher are providing this book and its contents on an "as is" basis and make no representations or warranties of any kind with respect to this book or its contents. The author and publisher disclaim all such representations and warranties, including, for example, warranties of merchantability and suitability for any particular purpose. In addition, the author and publisher do not represent or warrant that the information accessible via this book is accurate, complete, or current.

The statements made about policies, technology, and election systems have not been evaluated by any government agency. Please consult your legal, cybersecurity, or political expert regarding the implications and recommendations made in this book.

Except as expressly stated in this book, neither the author nor publisher nor any contributors or representatives will be liable for damages arising out of or in connection with the use of this book. This is a comprehensive limitation of liability that applies to all damages of any kind, including (without limitation) compensatory, direct, indirect, or consequential damages; loss of data, income, or profit; loss of or property damage; and claims of third parties.

You understand this book is not a substitute for consultation with licensed political, legal, or cybersecurity professionals. Before making any decisions or changes based on the content of this book, you should consult a licensed professional to ensure the best outcome for your situation.

This book is based on a doctoral study that takes a quantitative, non-experimental approach to examining the relationship between voters' belief in foreign election meddling and how it influences their decision-making process. Using the social cognitive theory as its framework, the research highlights the role of information sources in shaping voter perceptions, finding that those who relied on traditional news media rather than blogs or social media were more likely to recognize interference efforts. Use of this book implies your acceptance of this disclaimer.

Acknowledgment

Reflecting on my life's journey, I am deeply grateful for the winding path that has brought me to this moment. I am Faton Aliu, and my story is one of resilience, forged in adversity and sustained by the steady flame of hope.

Growing up, I witnessed the fierce struggle for freedom in my home country, Kosova. Under occupation, the indomitable will of the people shone brightly. With the support of allies like the USA, the UK, and others, our war for liberation became a defining chapter in history—a testament to the power of unity and unyielding perseverance.

Amidst the turmoil, education emerged as a beacon of hope and strength. It has been my guiding light, leading me to a future filled with limitless possibilities. Today, as the first in my family to earn a doctoral degree—an Executive Doctoral Degree in Business from Ecole des Ponts—I stand at the threshold of success, filled with pride and deep gratitude.

At the heart of my journey is the unwavering support of my family—my parents, Feti and Xhevrie, my brother Beli, my wife Arieta, and my children, Amisa and Jon. Their love and encouragement have been the foundation upon which my dreams have grown, and for that, I am forever thankful.

I would also like to express my deepest gratitude to my mentor, Dr. Nick Harkiolakis. His wisdom, patience, and steadfast belief in my potential have been instrumental in shaping my academic journey. To him, I offer my sincerest thanks.

My doctoral thesis, "Voters' Belief in Cyber Election Meddling and its Impact on their Decision-Making Process in Government Elections," is the culmination of years of research, reflection, and dedication. It represents my commitment to exploring the complex intersections of politics, technology, and democracy—a journey made richer through the guidance of Dr. Harkiolakis and the unwavering support of my loved ones.

As I embark on this next chapter, I invite you to join me in a quest for understanding, enlightenment, and positive change. This is not just my story—it is a reflection of the resilience of the human spirit, the transformative power of education, and the enduring legacy of those who dare to dream.

With sincere gratitude,
Dr. Faton Aliu

Abstract

While foreign actors have tried interfering with government elections, 2016 escalated to previously unseen levels. During the 2016 presidential election in the US, Russian state-sponsored organizations systematically spread misinformation across social media, news outlets, and surrogates. Subsequent investigations found that these cyber-influence campaigns damaged the public's trust in candidates and the electoral system, changing voter perceptions and decision-making processes. On the heels of these successful cyber-meddling efforts, Russia continued to influence other elections, such as those related to Brexit or the French governmental elections in 2017. The purpose of this quantitative, non-experimental correlational study was to provide an understanding of the relationship between voters' belief in cyber election meddling by foreign governments and their belief in its impact on their decision-making process in government elections. The population consisted of individuals who had voted in a national election since 2016. The social cognitive theory served as the theoretical framework for this study. The results of the study indicate that participants in this study were more likely to believe that election interference occurred through social media when they relied on information sources other than blog posts or social media alone. Furthermore, the findings of this study suggest that better-educated participants were more likely to claim that they have noticed cyber-meddling across media sources. Therefore, this study concluded that simply being aware of a disinformation campaign does not necessarily diminish its impact on voters' decision-making process.

Keywords: Cyber election meddling, government elections, voter perceptions, social cognitive theory, impacts on election decision-making, computational propaganda, foreign election interferences

Table of Contents

List of Tables

List of Figures

Chapter 1:
Introduction

One critical feature of a democratic country is the conduct of free elections at regular intervals as prescribed by the country's constitution. In recent decades, it has become increasingly common for some countries to engage in interference with foreign elections (Tomz & Weeks, 2020). Research conducted by the Centre for the Study of Democratic Institutions at the University of British Columbia has identified four principal techniques used by foreign actors to interfere in elections: (a) hacking attacks targeting systems, accounts, and databases to access, alter, or leak private information; (b) mass misinformation and propaganda campaigns that promote false, deceptive, biased, and inflammatory messages, often utilizing bots or fake social media accounts; (c) acquisition of data on populations or individuals to develop messages for micro-targeted manipulation; and (d) conducting online "trolling" operations to threaten, stigmatize, and harass individuals or groups (Tenove et al., 2018). While not all foreign actors may utilize these techniques to interfere with elections, the deployment of even one can significantly influence election outcomes (Baines & Jones, 2018; Schmitt, 2021). The U.S. Senate Select Committee on Intelligence (SSCI) undertook a bipartisan investigation into various Russian activities connected to the 2016 U.S. presidential election (Burr et al., 2018). The Committee completed a comprehensive examination of the Intelligence Community Assessment (ICA) issued by the Central

Intelligence Agency (CIA), National Security Agency (NSA), and Federal Bureau of Investigation (FBI) in January 2017 concerning Russian interference in the 2016 U.S. presidential election (Office of the Director of National Intelligence, 2017). Addressing the issue of Russian cyber-interference in the election, the former Acting Director of the Central Intelligence Agency, Michael Morell, remarked, "It is an attack on our very democracy. It is an attack on who we are as a people… this is to me not an overstatement; this is the political equivalent of 9/11" (Morell & Kelly, 2016). Numerous reports have suggested that the Russian State Intelligence Agency might have illegally accessed the Democratic National Committee's internal servers and collaborated with WikiLeaks to release a collection of internal emails on the eve of the Democratic convention (Fidler, 2016). The NSA, CIA, and the FBI compiled a joint report detailing Moscow's employment of cyber activities aimed at undermining the democracy of the United States, a move seen as predictable due to the prolonged Cold War history between the two nations (Office of the Director of National Intelligence, 2017). The report contains sections that evoke Cold War sentiments, highlighting Moscow's intent to weaken the US-led liberal democratic order. However, the report distinguishes the efforts in 2016 by noting a significant escalation in Russia's direct influence efforts and an expansion in the level and scope of its activities beyond those of past operations (Office of the Director of National Intelligence, 2017). With high confidence, the report also acknowledges the Russian government's execution of a sophisticated social media campaign aimed at influencing the 2016 elections. Reflecting on the intensified efforts to exert influence, Russian Prime Minister Dmitry Medvedev commented at a security conference in Munich, Germany, "Sometimes I wonder if it is the year 2016 or 1962" (Hjelmgaard, 2016).

A 2017 memorandum by the Federal Election Commission (FEC) highlighted the American public's alarm at widespread reports of foreign influence on the 2016 presidential election, leading to an expectation of federal government action in response to the security breach (Vigdor, 2019). Former U.S. Vice President Dick Cheney suggested that Russia's alleged interference could be viewed as an "act of war" (Cahill, 2017). Additionally, investigations into Russian interference extended beyond the U.S., with the UK Electoral Commission, the UK Parliament's Culture Select Committee, and the U.S. Senate examining alleged Russian meddling in the "Brexit" referendum of June 23, 2016 (Intelligence and Security Committee of Parliament, 2020). The "Russia Report," a comprehensive 55-page analysis of Russia's malign interference in UK politics, was crafted by an independent committee comprising nine Members of Parliament from various political parties, including the ruling Conservatives. This report outlined the UK's significant underestimation of the threat posed by Russian interference and the government's subsequent struggles to address this issue effectively, leading to attempts by the Johnson administration to delay its release (Ellehuus & Ruy, 2020). Although some may argue that the disinformation and influence campaigns surrounding Brexit were somewhat limited in scope, the presence of Russian influence within UK politics is expected to persist as Russia continues its cyber-meddling efforts (Intelligence and

Security Committee of Parliament, 2020). This pattern of behavior, similar to Russia's interference in the 2016 U.S. presidential elections, suggests a broader trend of manipulation that is likely to continue (Schia & Gjesvik, 2020). The report delineates that if Russia played a role in influencing the 2016 Brexit referendum, it was not via direct meddling in the voting process, which in the United Kingdom is conducted exclusively with paper ballots and is considered highly secure. Instead, the report points to the possibility that Moscow-based misinformation campaigns disseminated through social media platforms and Russian state-funded broadcasters like Sputnik and RT could have played a significant role in shaping public opinion (Ellehuus & Ruy, 2020). This strategy, along with the recruitment of influential public figures to echo certain narratives, akin to tactics observed during the 2016 U.S. presidential election, contributed to the creation of a potent alternative narrative (Ellehuus & Ruy, 2020; Grinberg et al., 2019; Schia & Gjesvik, 2020). The controversy known as the Macron Leaks, which involved the leak of over 20,000 emails associated with Macron's campaign in the days leading up to his victory in the 2017 election, represents another instance of election meddling (Downing & Ahmed, 2019). The 2017 French presidential election is notable not only for this leak of substantial amounts of hacked data on the eve of the vote, attributed to external efforts to influence the election outcome but also for highlighting the growing concern over the role of fake news in shaping electoral outcomes in democracies globally (Vilmer & Conley, 2018; Downing & Ahmed, 2019). In these cases, social media played a pivotal role in disseminating misinformation, underscoring its significant impact on public perception and democratic processes (Allcott & Gentzkow, 2017; Allcott et al., 2019; Downing & Ahmed, 2019; Ellehuus & Ruy, 2020; Wu et al., 2019).

Statement of the Problem

This research will address the specific problem that some voters lack an understanding of the relationship between their belief in cyber election meddling by foreign governments and its impact on their decision-making process in government elections (Baines & Jones, 2018; Sander, 2019). Ever since allegations of Russian meddling in the 2016 U.S. presidential election, cyber-influence operations have garnered worldwide attention. (Sander, 2019). The manipulation of voter perceptions is a major challenge to the legitimacy of elections (Wu et al., 2022). Following reports indicating the possibility of foreign cyber-meddling in the 2016 U.S. elections, voter perceptions may have been manipulated (Fidler, 2016). For example, the Internet Research Agency, LLC (IRA), a Russian organization funded by Yevgeniy Viktorovich Prigozhin, conducted social media operations targeted at large U.S. audiences to sow discord in the U.S. political system (Mueller, 2019a).

Furthermore, an investigation by the UK Electoral Commission, the UK Parliament's Culture Select Committee, alleged Russian interference in the "Brexit" poll of June 23, 2016 (Intelligence and Security Committee of Parliament, 2020). In particular, the report opens the possibility that Moscow-based information operations may have been a significant factor (Ellehuus & Ruy, 2020). Moreover, understanding how social media platforms impact public life is difficult (Bradshaw & Howard, 2018), and in some jurisdictions, spreading computational propaganda may be illegal (Howard et al., 2018). However, there is evidence that the strategies and techniques used by government cyber-troops have an impact and that their activities violate the norms of democratic practice (Howard et al., 2019).

Purpose of the Study

The purpose of this quantitative, non-experimental, cross-sectional, and correlational study was to provide an understanding of the relationship between voters' belief in cyber election meddling by foreign governments and their belief in its impact on their decision-making process in government elections. The population consisted of individuals who had voted in a national election since 2016. A minimum sample size of 115 participants was calculated using G*Power. The sample size calculation is based on an a priori power analysis for exact correlation, with correlation (p H1) of 0.30, $\alpha = 0.05$, and power of 95%. An online questionnaire was developed based on existing literature for data collection purposes and was validated through an initial pilot study. An invitation to participate was sent through LinkedIn's direct messaging system. Participation was voluntary and anonymous. The variables in this study included (a) voter perception of cyber election meddling by foreign governments and (b) voters' belief in its impact on their decision-making process. SPSS software version 28 was used to process the data and conduct the statistical analysis. Descriptive and inferential statistics were used to address the hypotheses and research questions of the study.

Theoretical Framework

The social cognitive theory (SCT) serves as the theoretical framework for this study. This theory posits that individuals learn and develop by observing others, acquiring information and skills through observation, and imitating others' behavior (Bandura & Walters, 1977). SCT emphasizes the role of social and environmental factors in shaping an individual's behavior and highlights the reciprocal relationship between cognitive, behavioral, and environmental variables (Bandura, 1986). This theory was deemed appropriate for this study as it sheds light on how individuals form attitudes and beliefs through observing and interpreting information from their social and physical environment. SCT suggests that attitudes and beliefs are shaped by direct personal experiences, as well as by indirect experiences, such as exposure to media, public opinion, and public discourse (Bandura, 1977), making it ideal for evaluating the reasons behind the voters' lack of understanding of how cyber election meddling by foreign governments may impact their voter decision-making process in government elections.

This study will examine the relationship between cyber-election meddling by foreign governments and their impact on the voter decision-making process in government elections. SCT provides a valuable framework for understanding how information from online sources can influence voter attitudes and beliefs and how these attitudes and beliefs can influence their vote and perception of the election outcomes. In particular, the theory suggests that the learning process includes several important factors, like (a) learning through observation, (b) paying attention, (c) retention, (d) reproduction, and (e) motivation (Figure 1). However, while these factors are important aspects of learning, they are also influenced by behavior, social environment, and personal traits, such as cognition, beliefs, and skills (Schunk & Usher, 2019). The interdependencies between behavior, personality, and the environment concerning the learning process make the SCT an ideal theoretical framework for investigating how cyber-meddling impacts self-evaluation, values, and outcome expectations in voters.

Figure 1. *Impact of Cyber-meddling on the voter decision-making process in national elections conceptual framework*

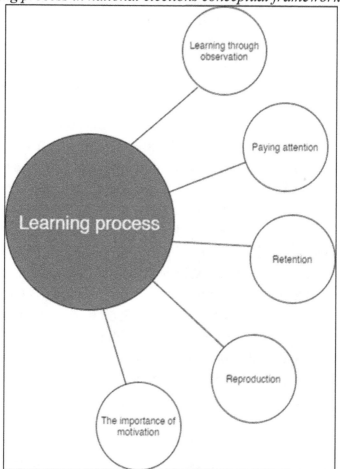

Nature of the Study

This study employs quantitative research methodology to examine the relationship between cyber election meddling by foreign governments and their impact on the voter decision-making process in government elections. Quantitative methods were deemed appropriate due to the need for statistical analysis of numerical data and hypothesis testing (Yilmaz, 2013). Quantitative research, emphasizing systematic measurement and statistical analysis, offers significant potential for generalizing findings across larger populations. By quantifying variables that describe the phenomenon under investigation, researchers can identify patterns, relationships, and trends beyond the specific sample studied (Savela, 2018; Yilmaz, 2013). This generalizability is achieved through rigorous sampling techniques and standardized data collection methods, ensuring that the results represent the target population (Abutabenjeh & Jaradat, 2018; Creswell, 2014). However, it is crucial to acknowledge the limitations of quantitative research, such as the potential for bias and the exclusion of contextual factors, which may impact the applicability of findings in certain situations. Nonetheless, the ability to generalize findings remains a crucial strength of quantitative research, enabling scholars to make inferences and predictions confidently.

The research design of this study is descriptive, non-experimental, and cross-sectional. Descriptive research provides a detailed description of variables and their characteristics, such as definitions, ranges, limitations, and units of measurement (Harkiolakis, 2017). The large amount of data generated by descriptive research helps make recommendations for practice (Moser & Korstjens, 2018; Savela, 2018; Taguchi, 2018). Delimitating the study subject to events related to and leading up to elections requires using a cross-sectional design, which captures a snapshot of the phenomenon and its interpretation at a specific time (Spector & Meier, 2014). Furthermore, this study focused on the population of voters in national elections, only including those who exercised their right to vote.

A non-probabilistic purposive sampling approach was employed, meaning that participants were selected based on specific criteria and qualifications to ensure a heterogeneous representation of the entire population. Participants were recruited through open invitations posted on Facebook, LinkedIn®, direct messaging, and email. Data was collected through an online questionnaire hosted on Google Forms, modeled after existing instruments previously used to measure perceptions and behaviors of participant attributes. The validity of the questionnaire was ensured through a review by a committee of experts and a pilot study. The data collected were analyzed using the Statistical Package for the Social Sciences (SPSS) version 28.

The statistical analysis included the one-sample chi-square test, the chi-square test for independence, and the Kruskal-Wallis test for variables that were not normally distributed. Spearman's rho was used to determine relationships and the strength of the relationships between the study variables. Furthermore, ethical and privacy issues were addressed as required by Ecole des Ponts Business School practices. Any surveys that were not fully completed were excluded from the analysis.

Research Questions

The following research question (RQ) guided the study:

RQ. Is there a relationship between voters' belief in cyber election meddling by foreign governments and their belief in its impact on their decision-making process in government elections?

Hypotheses

H_0: There is no relationship between voters' belief in cyber election meddling by foreign governments and their belief in its impact on their decision-making process in government elections.

H_a: There is a relationship between voters' belief in foreign governments' cyber election meddling and their belief in its impact on their decision-making process in government elections.

Significance of the Study

This study examines reported cyber-meddling and its effect on government elections like the 2016 U.S. Federal elections, the 2020 U.S. Federal elections, the 2016 Brexit referendum in the U.K., and the 2017 French presidential election. Against this background, this study determines whether cyber-meddling affected voters' decision-making process in election results. Furthermore, this study determined whether cyber-meddling impacted voters' perceptions of future elections. These findings may be crucial for shaping policies and interventions to restore trust in the electoral process.

Social media platforms play a significant role in shaping public opinion and facilitating communication. However, the rise of cyber-meddling has threatened the integrity and security of these platforms. The findings of this study can offer insights into how social media companies could implement robust measures for preventing election interference. Furthermore, the study's results could assist governments and policymakers in developing enforceable accounting strategies and mitigating the cyber-meddling threat in future elections on these platforms. Policymakers can use the results to create effective strategies for protecting future elections from cyber-meddling. At the same time, the public will be better informed about the risks posed by election interference on social media and the measures being taken to mitigate these risks. This study could represent an important step in restoring the public's trust in the electoral process and strengthening it for the years to come.

Definitions of Key Terms

Decision-making process: the cognitive and organizational procedures used by individuals and groups to evaluate alternatives, analyze risks, and determine the optimal course of action in various situations (Kahneman & Tversky, 1979).

Election Cyber-meddling refers to using computational technologies in cyberspace for malevolent and destructive purposes to transform, influence, or modify the election results for a particular country (Sander, 2019).

Government Elections: a recurring democratic process in which citizens vote to choose representatives and make decisions on public policies, guided by electoral systems and procedures (Powell & Powell Jr, 2000).

Voter perception: the subjective interpretation and understanding of political candidates, issues, and campaigns by individual voters, often influenced by various factors such as media, personal beliefs, and social interactions (Huddy et al., 2015).

Summary

Chapter 1 introduced some challenges that democracies continue to face with election meddling. The risk of election interference via new technologies and evolving tactics is a continuing challenge for democracies. As such, researchers, social media companies, and lawmakers must take steps to ensure that election meddling can be effectively addressed. It is essential to consider the attitudes and behaviors of voters exposed to such interference. Examining how election interference affects individuals' voting behavior may provide valuable information for creating more effective strategies and regulations to prevent future election meddling. For example, research may show that individuals subjected to deceptive ads or negative opinions on social media are more likely to change their voting behavior. By better understanding how voters process and use information from their social environment, researchers and lawmakers can develop more effective tools and policies to protect the integrity of democratic processes, including enacting laws that prevent or reduce the impact of future attempts at election interference.

This study examined the impact of election meddling on voters through the lens of the SCT. The SCT posits that individuals are heavily influenced by the information they receive from their social environment and that this information helps shape their attitudes, beliefs, and behaviors (Bandura & Walters, 1977). The population consisted of individuals who participated in a general election and were exposed to cyber-meddling. A descriptive, non-experimental, cross-sectional design was selected, and data collection relied on a self-administered survey instrument to gather participant data. A non-probabilistic purposive sampling method was employed to select participants from the identified population, ensuring that the participants were representative of the larger population of voters subjected to election meddling. Before collecting the data, a pilot study was conducted to verify the validity and reliability of the questionnaire used.

Chapter 2:
Literature Review

The purpose of this quantitative, non-experimental correlational study was to elucidate the relationship between voters' beliefs in cyber election interference by foreign governments and their perceptions of its influence on their decision-making processes in governmental elections. The research addresses voters' limited comprehension regarding the connection between their beliefs in foreign cyber election interference and its consequent impact on their decision-making processes in governmental elections (Baines & Jones, 2018; Sander, 2019). This review critically evaluates the existing literature on cyber-election interference and its significance to the voter decision-making process in governmental elections. The initial segment of the literature review focuses on the study's theoretical foundation, addressing the impact of cyber-election interference on voter perceptions. This portion further examines the multifaceted nature of the learning process and the influence of factors such as the environment, motivation, or individual characteristics on the decision-making process. Furthermore, the review delves into significant recent elections in the United States, the United Kingdom, and France, analyzing instances of cyber-election interference and their implications for voter perceptions. An overarching evaluation of motivational factors among voters in the United States, Europe, and other areas offers insights into the susceptibility of specific voter decision-making processes to cyber-election manipulation. The chapter concludes with a summary.

Literature Search Strategies

The search strategy for the literature review began with categorizing necessary search items into primary and secondary groups, which served as the basis for search keywords. The search initially utilized Google Scholar and was expanded to include multiple databases, such as JSTOR, ResearchGate, and EBSCO. Key search terms included "cyber-election interference," "voter perception," "decision-making processes," "social cognitive theory," "Brexit referendum," "US general elections," and "French presidential elections," among various combinations of these terms. Regarding frameworks and theories, terms such as "theory," "framework," "methodologies," "implementation," and "methods" were consistently applied throughout the research process. These additional searches enhanced the understanding of research across different areas and produced results that highlighted studies contesting prior works. The literature review thoroughly examines past cyber-election interference efforts by governments. It also explores techniques state-sponsored actors employ to manipulate elections and lists initiatives taken to prevent such interference in the future. Additionally, the review outlines common factors influencing voter decision-making across various jurisdictions. It specifically addresses differences in the voter decision-making process among Europe, the United States, and other nations.

Theoretical Framework

Exploring the learning process necessitates incorporating various theoretical perspectives to achieve a comprehensive understanding of the subject. One such perspective, Social Cognitive Theory (SCT), emphasizes the role of cognitive, behavioral, and environmental factors in learning (Bandura, 1986). This theory differs from other perspectives, such as the Theory of Planned Behavior (Ajzen, 1991), the Elaboration Likelihood Model (Cacioppo & Petty, 1986), the Social Learning Theory (Bandura & Walters, 1977), and the Theory of Self-Efficacy (Bandura, 1977). Developed by Bandura (1986), SCT offers a robust framework for examining the learning process. This theory posits that individuals acquire knowledge and skills through the interplay of personal, behavioral, and environmental factors. For instance, Schunk and DiBenedetto (2016) highlight the importance of self-efficacy, goal setting, and self-regulation in facilitating effective learning. Moreover, Bandura (1977) emphasized that observational learning underscores the significance of social and environmental influences in shaping individuals' learning experiences. SCT emerged in 1986 as a response to the limitations of behaviorism, which focused primarily on observable behaviors and external stimuli, often neglecting the role of cognition in the learning process. Bandura, a prominent psychologist, was a leading figure in the development of SCT, and his work on observational learning and self-efficacy significantly contributed to establishing this theory (Bandura, 1986). The beginnings of SCT can be traced back to Bandura's classic Bobo doll experiment in 1961, where he demonstrated the power of observational learning in shaping children's behaviors (Bandura & Walters, 1963). As the theory evolved, it started incorporating cognitive, environmental, and social factors that affect human behavior, thus providing a more comprehensive and holistic understanding of the learning process. The central tenets of SCT revolve around the reciprocal interactions among cognitive, behavioral, and environmental factors, a concept often referred to as "triadic reciprocal causation" (Bandura, 1986). This model posits that these three factors are interdependent and constantly influence one another, rendering them all essential components of the learning process. Key constructs within SCT include self-efficacy, which is an individual's belief in their ability to perform specific tasks or achieve particular goals, and observational learning, wherein individuals acquire new behaviors or knowledge by observing the actions of others (Bandura, 1977; Schunk, 1987). Furthermore, SCT emphasizes the importance of self-regulation—monitoring and controlling one's behaviors and cognitive processes—and goal setting, which involves establishing realistic and achievable objectives to guide one's actions. By integrating these aspects, SCT offers a comprehensive framework for understanding human learning and behavior (Bandura, 2001; Schunk & Usher, 2019; Zimmerman & Schunk, 2004), making it a valuable perspective for examining voter perception and the related decision-making process.

Figure 2. *Triadic Reciprocal Causation*

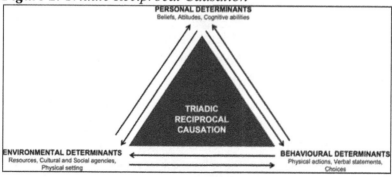

Learning through Observation: SCT posits that observational learning, also known as vicarious learning, is a crucial aspect of human development (Bandura, 1986). This concept emphasizes that individuals can acquire new knowledge and skills by observing the actions and consequences experienced by others without directly engaging in the behavior themselves (Bandura & Walters, 1977). Observational learning involves four main processes: attention, retention, reproduction, and motivation. These processes enable individuals to pay attention to the behaviors of others, remember the actions and outcomes, replicate the observed behaviors, and be motivated to perform those behaviors based on the observed consequences (Bandura, 1986). Several academic studies have applied the SCT concept of learning through observation in various contexts. Johnson et al. (2022) utilized SCT to investigate the impact of observing performance and receiving feedback on developing surgical skills among novice surgeons. The results demonstrated that students who received formative feedback from expert surgeons were more likely to effectively acquire and retain surgical skills and practice these skills at home. Another study explored the role of observational learning in developing children's self-efficacy and self-regulation in solving mathematical problems (Schunk, 1987). This study found that children who observed their peers successfully solving problems exhibited improved self-efficacy and self-regulation, leading to enhanced problem-solving abilities. These examples illustrate the powerful influence of observational learning in shaping human behavior and skill development across various domains.

Paying Attention. Regarding SCT, attention is a critical aspect of observational learning. In SCT, individuals acquire knowledge, skills, and behaviors by observing others and focusing on the relevant aspects of their actions (Bandura & Walters, 1977). Attention is the cognitive process that allows learners to selectively concentrate on specific aspects of the modeled behavior while ignoring irrelevant information (Bandura, 1977). Furthermore, this process is essential for encoding the observed behavior and subsequently reproducing it. Attention is influenced by various factors, including the observer's cognitive abilities, motivation, and the salience of the observed behavior.

Recently, researchers have begun applying the SCT concept of paying attention to learning through social media exposure. For example, Alwagait et al. (2015) investigated the impact of social media on students' academic performance, highlighting the significance of attention in online learning environments. Additionally, Yoon and Tourassi (2014) explored the role of attention in learning through social networking sites, specifically focusing on how the design and features of these platforms influence attentional processes. Both studies underscore the critical role of paying attention in observational learning, particularly in social media contexts, where learners are exposed to various stimuli that may compete for their attention.

Retention. Retention is a crucial component of the SCT, as it involves the ability of an individual to remember and store observed behaviors, experiences, and information for future use (Bandura & Walters, 1977). This process significantly shapes individuals' decision-making by enabling them to recall past experiences and modify their actions accordingly. Retention involves cognitive processes such as encoding, storage, and retrieval of information, which are essential for learning and subsequent behavioral change (Bandura, 1977). It serves as the mental repository from which individuals can draw when making decisions and adapting to new situations (Bandura, 1986). Several researchers have applied the SCT concept of retention to the decision-making process. Bandura and Walters (1963) investigated the impact of retention on aggressive behavior in children, highlighting the role of observational learning and memory in shaping their choices. A subsequent study by Lent, Brown, and Hackett (2007) examined the influence of self-efficacy, outcome expectations, and retention on academic satisfaction among college students. This research emphasized the importance of retaining self-efficacy beliefs and outcome expectations in guiding students' academic satisfaction and their ability to make informed decisions. Both studies illustrate the significance of retention within SCT in understanding how individuals make decisions based on their past experiences, observations, and internalized information.

Reproduction. Reproduction, within the context of Social Cognitive Theory (SCT), refers to the process of translating learned information into action (Bandura & Walters, 1977). This process involves replicating observed behaviors or skills and applying them in different situations. Reproduction is a critical component of the learning process, as it enables individuals to practice and refine their newly acquired skills, thereby facilitating long-term mastery. SCT posits that successful reproduction depends on various factors, including self-efficacy, cognitive rehearsal, and feedback. These elements collectively shape an individual's ability to accurately perform a learned behavior (Bandura, 1977, 1986; Bandura & Walters, 1977).

Several academic papers have explored the reproduction concept within SCT and its impact on outcomes. Bandura (2018) applied SCT to investigate the role of self-efficacy in promoting health behaviors, suggesting that individuals with higher self-efficacy were more likely to reproduce health-promoting behaviors, leading to improved outcomes. Similarly, Zimmerman and Schunk (2004) examined the effects of self-regulatory processes, including reproduction, on academic performance. Their research revealed that students who effectively employed self-regulatory processes, such as setting goals and monitoring progress, demonstrated better reproduction of learning strategies and subsequently achieved higher academic outcomes. Both studies underscore the importance of reproduction in facilitating the successful application of learned behaviors and demonstrate its impact on various outcomes.

Motivation. The SCT posits that motivation is a crucial driving force influencing an individual's actions and behaviors.

Furthermore, motivation results from the complex interplay between cognitive, behavioral, and environmental factors (Bandura & Walters, 1977). Central to this concept is self-efficacy, which refers to an individual's belief in their ability to accomplish a specific task or achieve a desired outcome (Bandura, 1977). This belief influences their motivation to engage in behaviors that align with their goals. For instance, a person with high self-efficacy in influencing political outcomes may be more motivated to participate in voting (Caprara et al., 2009). Within SCT, motivation is also influenced by factors such as observational learning, goal setting, and self-regulation, which collectively contribute to an individual's decision-making process (Bandura, 2018; Bandura & Walters, 1977; Zimmerman & Schunk, 2004).

Several academic papers have applied the concept of motivation from the SCTs to the voter decision-making process in elections. Wu et al. (2022) suggested that social cognitive factors like perception can influence voter motivation and outcomes. In another study, Velasquez and Quenette (2018) examined the impact of social media exposure on political engagement. Their findings suggest that social cognitive factors, including political self-efficacy and political interest, mediated the relationship between social media exposure and voting behavior. These studies underscore the importance of understanding how motivation, derived from SCT, plays a significant role in shaping voter decision-making during elections.

The Impact of Behavior, Social Environment, and Personal Traits. The interplay of behavior, social environment, and personal traits shapes human learning and behavior, serving as essential tenets of the SCT (Bandura & Walters, 1977). These elements constitute a triadic reciprocal causation, where changes in one aspect lead to adjustments in the others. For example, observing others in their social environment can influence an individual's behavior, thus shaping their personal beliefs and attitudes. In learning, SCT emphasizes the importance of observational learning, self-regulation, and self-efficacy, all influenced by the individual's behavior, social environment, and personal traits (Bandura, 1977 1986; Bandura & Walters, 1963, 1977). These concepts elucidate how individuals acquire and apply new knowledge and skills in daily life. In political science, researchers have applied SCT to understand the voter decision-making process during elections. McDevitt and Kiousis (2006) explored the impact of media coverage on young voters' political engagement and decision-making, showing that exposure to mediated political content influenced their attitudes and behaviors during elections. Similarly, Bandura (2001) discussed the role of mass communication and social modeling in shaping voter behavior and opinions. Both studies demonstrate the applicability of SCT's concepts of behavior, social environment, and personal traits in understanding the complexities of the voter decision-making process, highlighting the theory's value in analyzing various aspects of human learning and behavior.

Theoretical Implications. The SCT provides a comprehensive framework for investigating voter decision-making by emphasizing the interplay between individual behavior, personal traits, and the social environment. Utilizing SCT allows researchers to explore the multifaceted nature of political decision-making, taking into account various factors such as political awareness, social influences, and exposure to political media (Bandura, 2001; Schunk & Usher, 2019; Velasquez & Quenette, 2018; Zimmerman & Schunk, 2004). In this context, Pingree et al. (2014) examined the impact of political advertising on voter decision-making, finding that voters' cognitive processes and attitudes toward political campaigns were influenced by their perception of social norms and the opinions of others. Another theoretical implication of utilizing the SCT for investigating the voter decision-making process is its emphasis on the role of self-efficacy in shaping behavior. Self-efficacy, or an individual's belief in their ability to perform a specific task, can significantly impact voting behavior by influencing one's motivation and participation in the electoral process. In their study, Valentino et al. (2009) examined the moderating influence of self-efficacy on the relationship between negative political advertising and voter turnout. They found that individuals with high self-efficacy were more likely to vote even when exposed to negative advertisements. Studies like this underscore the importance of considering self-efficacy when examining voter decision-making processes, as it can help identify potential barriers to political participation.

Lastly, SCT's emphasis on observational learning provides valuable insights into how the voter decision-making process may be influenced by exposure to political information and the behaviors of others. Klofstad et al. (2013) investigated the role of social influence in shaping political discussions, demonstrating that individuals were more likely to engage in political conversations when they observed others doing so. This aspect of observational learning suggests that exposure to political discussions, whether in person or through media, can significantly impact voters' decision-making by shaping their political knowledge, opinions, and attitudes. Therefore, understanding the impact of observational learning, a key component of SCT, may offer a deeper understanding of voter decisions and the factors influencing their choices during elections.

Supporting Theories

SCT is underpinned by various psychological theories, including Social Learning Theory (SLT) and self-efficacy theory. SLT, proposed by Albert Bandura, highlights the significance of observing and modeling the behaviors, attitudes, and emotional reactions of others, aligning with SCT's emphasis on the role of the social environment in shaping behavior (Bandura, 1977; Bandura & Walters, 1977). Furthermore, Bandura's theory of self-efficacy, which suggests that an individual's belief in their ability to perform specific tasks influences their motivation, perseverance, and eventual success, complements SCT's focus on personal traits and their impact on behavior (Bandura, 1977). Although both theories contribute to understanding the complex interplay between individual, social, and environmental factors, they collectively underpin the tenets of SCT. Therefore, SCT is particularly suitable for investigating the relationship between voter belief in cyber election meddling by foreign governments and its perceived impact on their decision-making process in government elections.

Relevant Theories

Although SCT provides a comprehensive framework for understanding human behavior, other theories offer alternative perspectives. For instance, the Theory of Planned Behavior (TPB) emphasizes the role of attitudes, subjective norms, and perceived behavioral control in predicting individuals' intentions and actions (Ajzen, 1991). TPB suggests that an individual's behavior is directly influenced by their intentions, which are shaped by their attitudes towards the behavior, the social pressure they perceive, and their perceived ability to perform the behavior. Another significant theory is the Elaboration Likelihood Model (ELM) of persuasion, focusing on the cognitive processes involved in changing attitudes (Cacioppo & Petty, 1986). ELM proposes that persuasive messages are processed through either a central or peripheral route, depending on the individual's motivation and ability to engage in effortful cognitive processing. While TPB and ELM provide valuable insights into the complex interplay of attitudes, intentions, social influences, and mental processes in shaping human behavior, SCT emphasizes the importance of self-efficacy and observational learning. Therefore, SCT was deemed most suitable for investigating the relationship between voter belief in cyber election meddling by foreign governments and its perceived impact on their decision-making process in government elections.

Cyber Election Meddling by Foreign Governments

The voter decision-making process in government elections is complex and multifaceted, influenced by a variety of factors that shape an individual's political preferences and choices.

These factors can include personal values, political ideology, socioeconomic background, education, and the influence of mass media, among others. Voters may rely on a combination of cognitive shortcuts, such as party identification and issue voting, to simplify the decision-making process (Kanev, 2017; Wu et al., 2022). Additionally, emotions and personal experiences can significantly influence a voter's choice, with some individuals prioritizing issues that directly impact their lives or resonate with their core values (Marquart et al., 2020). With the widespread adoption of the internet, social media platforms and targeted advertising have become significant factors in shaping voter decision-making. Malicious actors may use social media to spread disinformation, sow discord, and create echo chambers that reinforce existing biases, ultimately influencing voter behavior (Agrawal, 2020; Ellehuus & Ruy, 2020; Garrett, 2019; Grinberg et al., 2019; Wong, 2019; Wu et al., 2019). Furthermore, political campaigns increasingly rely on micro-targeting strategies, leveraging data analytics to customize messages for specific demographic groups or individuals. These targeted efforts can sway undecided voters or suppress voter turnout by capitalizing on issues that resonate with them (Allcott et al., 2019; Benkler et al., 2018; Lewis & Hilder, 2018; Ohlin, 2020). Thus, understanding and addressing the various factors that influence the voter decision-making process is critical to ensuring the integrity of elections and the health of democratic institutions.

Since the 2016 US general election, cyber election meddling by foreign governments has emerged as a significant concern, threatening the fabric of democracy (Baines & Jones, 2018).

These malicious actors employ sophisticated tactics, such as spreading disinformation, hacking into electoral systems, and orchestrating targeted social media campaigns, to influence voters' decisions and undermine public trust in the democratic process (Burr et al., 2018; Downing & Ahmed, 2019; Ellehuus & Ruy, 2020). The consequences of such interference can be far-reaching, skewing election outcomes and eroding citizens' faith in their political institutions. In response to this growing challenge, governments, and technology companies have begun to collaborate and develop countermeasures to safeguard electoral integrity and protect the democratic values that underpin societies (Burr et al., 2018; Hicks, 2018; Norris, 2016; Sander, 2019).

US General Election in 2016

In the United States, voter decision-making encompasses various factors influencing their choices when casting ballots. A critical factor is political ideology, which often dictates voters' preferences for particular candidates or parties. Typically, voters with conservative leanings support Republican candidates, while those with liberal or progressive inclinations lean toward Democratic candidates (Frimer et al., 2017; Morris, 2020). The political ideology of a voter is often shaped by factors such as family, upbringing, education, and social background, ultimately guiding their perspectives on various political issues. However, the impact of cyber-election meddling during the US 2016 general election underscored the vulnerabilities of modern democracies to digital attacks and disinformation campaigns. A notable instance of proven interference was the hacking of the

Democratic National Committee's (DNC) email server by a Russian military intelligence unit (Banks, 2017). This breach resulted in the release of sensitive internal communications on websites like WikiLeaks, inflicting significant reputational damage on the Democratic Party and its presidential candidate, Hillary Clinton (Mueller, 2019). Additionally, Russia's Internet Research Agency (IRA) launched a well-coordinated disinformation campaign across social media platforms, including Facebook, Twitter, and Instagram. These efforts aimed to sow discord and polarize the American public by creating and promoting politically divisive content, amplifying existing social and political tensions (Howard et al., 2019; Ruck et al., 2019). The revelation of these cyberattacks and disinformation campaigns had far-reaching consequences on American politics and beyond. The US government and other nations began to take cyber threats more seriously and invested heavily in improving their cybersecurity infrastructure (Whyte, 2020). Social media platforms faced increased scrutiny and were urged to introduce measures to counter disinformation and foreign influence in their networks (Allcott & Gentzkow, 2017; Allcott et al., 2019). These events also led to a broader conversation about the role of social media in shaping public opinion and the importance of media literacy in the digital age (Agrawal, 2020; Benkler et al., 2018). In the years following the 2016 general election, there has been a growing awareness of election interference, and efforts have been made to bolster cybersecurity (Arquilla & Guzdial, 2017; Baram et al., 2017), enhance transparency (Robinson et al., 2015; Rundle, 2022), and promote accurate information in the political discourse (Giglietto et al., 2016; Peters, 2017; Sharma, 2017).

However, addressing cyber-election meddling remains an ongoing concern for democracies worldwide.

The UK Brexit Referendum in 2016

In Europe, voters' decision-making processes are influenced by various factors, including political ideologies, party loyalties, and regional affiliations. The European political landscape is characterized by multiple political parties catering to diverse segments of society. This diversity enables European voters to align themselves with parties representing their values and interests, significantly influencing their electoral choices. Additionally, European voters often prioritize social welfare, environmental policies, and international cooperation, reflecting the continent's historical emphasis on social democracy and multilateralism (Harrison, 2018; Van Elsas et al., 2019). The impact of cyber-election meddling during the UK 2016 Brexit referendum was significant, with foreign actors aiming to manipulate public opinion and sway the vote in their favor. A notable example of proven interference involved Russia, which deployed a network of social media accounts and bots to spread disinformation, amplify divisive content, and create confusion among voters (Cadwalladr & Graham-Harrison, 2018). These accounts targeted both Leave and Remain supporters, exploiting existing tensions in British society and fueling the polarized nature of the Brexit debate (Ellehuus & Ruy, 2020). Furthermore, investigations revealed that the Internet Research Agency, a Russian-based organization with ties to the Kremlin, played a crucial role in orchestrating these online campaigns (Farkas & Bastos, 2018). During the Brexit referendum, another tactic used was the employment of data analytics by political organizations other than British political parties to target voters with personalized digital advertisements. The controversial data-mining firm Cambridge Analytica was implicated in the Leave campaign for utilizing data obtained from millions of Facebook users without their consent (Waterson, 2018; Wong, 2019). This data enabled the firm to craft highly targeted ads aimed at swaying undecided voters towards the Leave side. The revelation of these strategies led to questions about the legitimacy of the Brexit vote and highlighted the susceptibility of democratic processes to cyber-election meddling. Consequently, there has been an increasing demand for enhanced transparency and regulation to preserve the integrity of elections and protect the democratic process from the influence of malicious actors (Schmitt, 2021; Schmitt & Watts, 2021).

French Presidential Election in 2017

In contrast to the polarized political landscape in the United States, which is primarily dominated by two major parties, the Democrats and the Republicans, French citizens are accustomed to a multi-party system. American voters often base their electoral decisions on their identification with one of these parties and their respective ideologies. In contrast, French voters have the option to choose among approximately 50 nationwide represented parties, in addition to many others that only operate at the local government level. While some issues, such as the economy, healthcare, and national security, resonate with voters across both continents, the framing of these issues can differ significantly in the US context. For example, American voters may prioritize individual liberties and a free-market economy more than European voters, who might favor government interventions and social safety nets (Braun & Tausendpfund, 2020; Okolikj & Quinlan, 2016). This divergence in political values and priorities underscores the key differences between Europe and the US regarding voter decision-making. During the French 2017 Presidential Election, cyber election meddling significantly impacted the political landscape and voter perceptions, with Emmanuel Macron's campaign being a primary target. In May 2017, just days before the final round of voting, a substantial cyberattack known as "MacronLeaks" occurred. Hackers infiltrated the campaign's email servers and leaked approximately 9 gigabytes of data, including private emails and documents, in an attempt to discredit Macron and sway public opinion in favor of his opponent, Marine Le Pen (Downing & Ahmed, 2019). The timing of the attack was particularly critical, as it took place during the election silence period, complicating the Macron campaign's ability to respond effectively. Although no direct link was established, suspicions pointed towards Russia as the potential perpetrator, given the similarities between the MacronLeaks attack and the interference in the US 2016 general election (Bollmann & Gibeon, 2022; Vilmer & Conley, 2018). In addition to the high-profile data leak, the French 2017 Presidential Election witnessed other forms of cyber election meddling. Social media platforms, especially Twitter, disseminated disinformation and inflammatory content to undermine Macron's credibility while supporting Le Pen's campaign (Bollmann & Gibeon, 2022; Bradshaw et al., 2017; Gaumont et al., 2018). Coordinated networks of bots and trolls were deployed to manipulate public discourse and emphasize divisive narratives. These tactics fostered increased skepticism and distrust among the French electorate, leading some voters to question the integrity of the democratic process. Although Macron ultimately won the election, the impact of cyber election meddling on public opinion and voter behavior during the French 2017 Presidential Election underscores the critical need for robust cybersecurity measures and heightened vigilance against foreign interference in democratic processes (Downing & Ahmed, 2019).

US General Election in 2020

A significant aspect of voter decision-making is the influence of media and information sources. With the advent of the internet and social media platforms, voters in the US have access to an extensive array of information that can shape their political choices. Traditional media outlets, such as newspapers, television, and radio, continue to play a crucial role in forming public opinion. However, social media has emerged as a potent tool for disseminating information, with many voters relying on these platforms to stay informed about political issues and candidates (Benkler et al., 2018; Bradshaw & Howard, 2018; Kalsnes, 2018; Kumar & Shah, 2018; Lysenko & Brooks, 2018). Consequently, voters are exposed to a wide range of perspectives and opinions, which can either reinforce their existing beliefs or challenge them, ultimately influencing their voting decisions (Alashri et al., 2016; Kanev, 2017; Sullo, 2020; Wu et al., 2022). The impact of cyber-election meddling during the US 2020 general election was significant, as foreign actors employed various tactics to influence the outcome and undermine public trust in the electoral process. A notable example of interference involved the indictment of two Iranian nationals for hacking a US media company and creating and disseminating disinformation (Department of Justice, 2021). Furthermore, Russian actors were identified as spreading disinformation through social media platforms, amplifying divisive narratives, and promoting conspiracy theories to sow discord among the American public (Ohlin, 2020). In response to these threats, the US government and private sector organizations took extensive measures to ensure the integrity of the 2020 election. Cybersecurity agencies, such as the Cybersecurity and Infrastructure Security Agency (CISA), work closely with state and local election officials to identify vulnerabilities in electoral systems and provide guidance on best practices for securing critical infrastructure (Rosenzweig, 2020; Stedmon, 2020). Social media platforms also played a vital role in combating foreign interference by implementing policies to flag and remove false or misleading content and suspending accounts linked to foreign disinformation campaigns (Ohlin, 2020; Stedmon, 2020). Despite these efforts, the persistence of cyber-election meddling in the 2020 US general election underscores the ongoing challenge of securing democratic processes against foreign interference and highlights the need for continued vigilance and investment in cybersecurity measures (Rundle, 2022; Schia & Gjesvik, 2020; Schmitt & Watts, 2021).

Other Jurisdictions and Elections

In many countries outside of Europe and the US, the voter decision-making process is influenced by a unique set of factors specific to their cultural, social, and political context. One such factor is the prominence of religious beliefs and affiliations, which can significantly shape voters' political preferences. For example, religious identity often intersects with political ideology in countries like India, Pakistan, and Indonesia, leading voters to support parties or candidates that align with their religious values (Choudhary et al., 2020; Said et al., 2021). This contrasts with the more secular politics in Europe and the US, where religious affiliations tend to have a lesser impact on voter behavior. Another factor affecting voters' decision-making process in non-European and non-US countries is the prevalence of patronage politics and clientelism, whereby politicians provide material benefits to their constituents in exchange for political support. This practice is particularly common in regions like Latin America, Africa, and Asia, where weak institutions and high levels of corruption create an environment where voters may prioritize immediate personal gains over long-term policy objectives (Kaltwasser & Van Hauwaert, 2020; Rennó, 2020). In contrast, European and US voters emphasize policy platforms and ideological stances when making electoral decisions, reflecting a more robust tradition of social democracy and institutional stability within these regions.

Summary

Cyber election meddling and voter perception have become important factors during recent government elections. Today, state-sponsored actors and other malicious groups use tactics such as misinformation campaigns and hacking into voting systems to manipulate election outcomes. Successful cyber-meddling during US, UK, and French elections suggests that these threats continue to evolve. Governments and organizations must work diligently to counteract them and protect the integrity of elections.

Most importantly, voter perception plays a pivotal role in the success of cyber-election meddling efforts. By exploiting voters' cognitive biases, bad actors can influence their decision-making process and alter the course of elections. Understanding the psychological and social factors that shape voter perception is essential for developing effective countermeasures against cyber-election meddling. It is crucial to explore relevant theoretical frameworks and methodologies to understand election cyber meddling and voter perception comprehensively. Additionally, examining the motivators for decision-making among voters in various jurisdictions can shed light on the differences in vulnerability to cyber-election meddling efforts.

Furthermore, the growing prevalence of cyber-election meddling and its impact on voter perception demands urgent attention. At this point, it is unclear if voters perceive cyber meddling and choose to ignore the attempt or its implied outcome. Although interference in the US 2016 and 2020 presidential elections, the French 2017 election, and the UK Brexit referendum have been well-documented, many voters still seem to fall victim to the same disinformation tactics used by state-sponsored actors. By further examining the methods used in election interference and the factors that influence voter perception, governments and organizations can develop more robust strategies to safeguard election integrity and improve voter confidence.

Chapter 3:
Research Method

This research aimed to address the specific problem that voters lack an understanding of the relationship between their belief in cyber election meddling by foreign governments and its impact on their decision-making process in government elections (Baines & Jones, 2018; Sander, 2019). The purpose of this quantitative, non-experimental, correlational study was to provide an understanding of the relationship between voters' belief in cyber election meddling by foreign governments and their belief in its impact on their decision-making process in government elections. This section delves into the quantitative research approach, encompassing the study's population, sample, and chosen materials and instruments. Additionally, this section provides a comprehensive definition of variables, an overview of the study's procedures, data gathering and evaluation, ethical considerations and assurances, and a discussion on assumptions, constraints, and boundaries before concluding with a summary.

Research Methodology and Design

Researchers who want to evaluate numerical data systematically employ quantitative methodologies (Park & Park, 2016). These methods are optimal for scrutinizing hypotheses and investigating connections between factors (House, 2018). Moreover, quantitative research techniques permit examining individual data associated with extensive populations, generalizing results, and establishing cause-and-effect relationships (Savela, 2018). Given that the objective of the current study was to explore the association between the research variables within a specific yet nonlocalized population, a quantitative research approach was deemed most suitable.

On the other hand, qualitative research methodologies hinge on the researcher's interpretation and do not stem from quantitative or statistical origins (Yilmaz, 2013). This type of research delves into the investigation of various phenomena, encompassing individuals, groups, methods, processes, or behaviors. It is ideally suited to comprehend lived experiences but falls short in identifying relationships between variables (Rutberg & Bouikidis, 2018). Generally, qualitative research is inductive and allows for inference without imposing preconceived notions on the investigator or the environment (Wark & Webber, 2015). This study aimed to quantify the link between the research variables and test hypotheses, so the qualitative research method was considered unsuitable.

Mixed methods research integrates quantitative and qualitative methodologies, allowing investigators to merge experiential knowledge and comprehensive, illustrative, and empirical data within one investigation (Schrauf, 2017). Researchers employ mixed methods research to integrate multiple methodologies when a single approach is inadequate for elucidating or exploring the phenomena of interest (Schoonenboom, 2018). Additionally, mixed methods can enhance the credibility of research findings, especially when relying on one method would yield limited data. By amalgamating information from diverse methods, triangulation frequently fuses qualitative and quantitative data, providing a more comprehensive understanding of the phenomenon from various viewpoints (Flick, 2016). However, since this study focused on measuring relationships among quantitative variables without requiring a qualitative component, mixed methods research was considered unsuitable.

Consequently, a correlational, non-experimental, and cross-sectional research design was chosen for this investigation. Descriptive research designs examine phenomena by utilizing or developing instruments to gauge variables (Wark & Webber, 2015). In contrast to explanatory research, which strives to uncover cause and effect connections, descriptive designs can yield practical recommendations due to the substantial volume of data frequently gathered through these methods (Park & Park, 2016; Yilmaz, 2013). On the other hand, exploratory designs assist researchers in comprehending a problem and its underlying concepts, often serving as a foundation for subsequent studies (Park & Park, 2016). Since this study aimed to generate practical suggestions rather than simply identifying cause and effect relationships between research variables or exploring constructs within the voter decision-making process, employing a descriptive design was deemed most fitting.

Moreover, as this study aimed to pinpoint disparities and traits among participants during the investigation, a cross-sectional design was considered most suitable. In contrast to longitudinal research designs, which examine the effects of changes over extended periods by sampling participants at regular intervals to identify evolving responses, cross-sectional methods concentrate on individual impressions from each participant at a single point in time (Spector & Meier, 2014).

Consequently, longitudinal designs are not ideal for making practical suggestions for future approaches until the change has occurred, making it unsuitable as a study design for this research.

One benefit of experimental designs is that they allow researchers to examine causality, meaning whether one action leads to another (Podsakoff & Podsakoff, 2018). Generally, there are two approaches to experimental designs: the first involves monitoring a variable over time to assess the impact of events, while the second entails observing variables before and after an event to determine if and how one might affect the other (Kazdin, 2018). Additionally, quasi-experimental designs can integrate multiple measures or control groups to study better cause-and-effect relationships (Podsakoff & Podsakoff, 2018). Although some regard experimental designs as more scientific than non-experimental research, experimental studies often face significant issues with external validity, as some investigations detach their experimental environments from reality (East, 2015). As this research did not aim to establish causality or manipulate variables, a non-experimental design was the most appropriate choice for conducting this study.

Population and Sample

The population consisted of individuals who had voted in a national election since 2016. The purpose of this quantitative, non-experimental correlational study was to provide an understanding of the relationship between voters' belief in cyber election meddling by foreign governments and their belief in its impact on their decision-making process in government elections. In particular, to measure the relationships between voters' perception of cyber-election meddling by foreign governments and their belief in its impact on their decision-making process in government elections, the relevant population primarily consisted of voters in recent national elections to ensure better recollection of perceived cyber-meddling. Furthermore, only those individuals who had cast a vote were included to examine whether perceived cyber-meddling impacted their decision-making process. Voters who did not cast a ballot were excluded from the population in this study.

In this study, a non-random purposive sampling technique was employed. Non-random purposive samples are frequently utilized by researchers who aim to select participants that align with predetermined demographic criteria (Jager et al., 2017). Although researchers screen participants to ensure a sample reflects the target population, excessive selectiveness can lead to participant bias and reduced variance (Costanza et al., 2015). Consequently, the research findings may not apply to a broader population unless the researcher maintains diversity (Zyphur & Pierides, 2017). Nevertheless, the generalizability of research outcomes may be restricted without a representative sample (Costanza et al., 2015). Enhancing the generalizability of non-probability sampling can be achieved by confirming that the purposive sample is representative of the population (Jager et al., 2017). Individuals from numerous jurisdictions could be chosen by not confining participants to a specific location, promoting the inclusion of diverse perceptions related to cyber-meddling and its impact on the voter decision-making process.

G*Power software was employed to determine the necessary sample size for the target population (Mayr et al., 2007). An

Exact-Test (correlation) was selected for this computation. Bivariate correlation is favored among researchers to investigate relationships due to its simplicity and capability to replace more complex tests (Bagya Lakshmi et al., 2018). A correlation size (p H1 = .30) and α = .05 was presumed for the a priori power analysis, suggesting a minimum sample size of 67 participants to achieve a power of .80. By augmenting the sample size to 115, the power could be increased to .95. Consequently, this investigation aimed to involve between 67 and 115 participants (Figure 3).

Figure 3. *Power as a function of sample size*

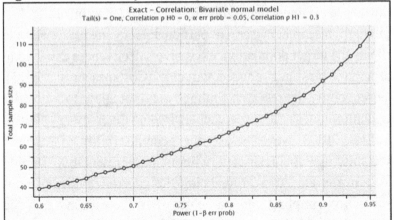

Materials/Instrumentation

In this study, data collection was performed using a survey tool. The questionnaire was crafted to evaluate voter beliefs concerning cyber meddling and its potential influence on their choices during governmental elections since 2016. Researchers typically pose questions for two purposes: (a) to address their research inquiries or (b) to determine the eligibility of study participants (Hughes et al., 2016). As such, the survey included eight demographic questions, such as jurisdiction, age, and voting history. Additionally, eleven questions assessed voter beliefs toward perceived cyber interference and participants' decision-making during governmental elections since 2016. These queries aimed to address the research objectives or further establish participant eligibility.

In this study concerning the perception of cyber interference and its influence on respondents' decision-making during a recent government election, a 5-point Likert scale was employed. Likert scales are frequently used in social science research for gauging attitudes and serve as effective measurement tools (Fogarty et al., 2016). Moreover, the survey used in this research was validated, initially drawing from pertinent research questions and constructs identified in the existing literature. Experts in research methodology and design, such as Dr. Harkiolakis from Ecole des Ponts and Dr. Thurman from Columbia University, provided feedback on the initial draft, which informed subsequent refinements and a pilot study to confirm the instrument's relevance and validity. When the data revealed inconsistencies, necessary adjustments were made to the survey before proceeding (Streitwieser et al., 2019). No modifications were required during the main study's data collection for questions demonstrating the instrument's strong validity. Further information about the pilot study and the survey can be found in Appendix A.

Operational Definitions of Variables
Cyber-Meddling (CM)

CM in elections refers to the deliberate use of digital tools and methods to manipulate, interfere, or disrupt the electoral process (Sander, 2019). This includes spreading disinformation, hacking into voting systems, and targeting political campaigns or candidates to influence public opinion (Schia & Gjesvik, 2020). CM aims to undermine the integrity of elections and create doubt about the legitimacy of their outcomes (Ellehuus & Ruy, 2020; Hasen, 2017). The operational definition involves identifying specific tactics, such as social media manipulation, cyber-attacks on infrastructure, and unauthorized access to sensitive information. CM concerns were treated as a predictive interval-level variable, measured using a 5-point Likert-type scale (1=strongly disagree to 5= strongly agree).

Voter Decision-making (VDM)

VDM processes refer to individuals' cognitive steps and considerations as they form their preferences and cast their ballots in an election. These processes begin with acquiring information about candidates, parties, and policies, often influenced by personal values, beliefs, and social context (Wu et al., 2022). Voters then evaluate their options, comparing and contrasting each candidate's positions, qualifications, and trustworthiness. Following this evaluation, individuals make a choice, selecting the candidate or party they believe best aligns with their interests and priorities (Kanev, 2017; Marquart et al., 2020; McDevitt & Kiousis, 2006; Okolikj & Quinlan, 2016; Said et al., 2021; Van Elsas et al., 2019). Finally, voters act on their decisions by participating in the electoral process through traditional in-person voting, mail-in ballots, or online platforms, ultimately influencing the election outcome. VDM was a predictor interval-level variable measured through a 5-point Likert-type scale (1=*strongly disagree to 5= strongly agree*). This variable was assessed through survey questions one to eleven.

Data Collection and Analysis

The data collection process was conducted anonymously via an online survey hosted on Google Forms. Participants were reached through email or direct messaging, and essential information about the study was shared with them before they responded to any questions. Utilizing web-based questionnaires and email communication for participant recruitment and survey administration is more cost-effective than other methods, such as conventional mail (Ebert et al., 2018). However, online surveys may experience lower response rates, potentially reducing the effective sample size and impacting the statistical power of the gathered data (Loomis & Paterson, 2018).

To enhance response rates, researchers can often surpass this limitation and achieve greater than average response rates by meticulously crafting messages for participant contact and tailoring the survey to the target audience instead of merely depending on templates (Burke & Hodgins, 2015). As a result, personalized messages and follow-ups were integrated into the recruitment strategy for this study. A maximum of three messages and follow-ups were sent to each participant as part of the direct messaging part of recruitment, allowing at least one week to elapse between these reminder cycles. Despite the customized communication efforts, several participants had to be disqualified because of invalid responses, necessitating contact with additional eligible individuals to attain the desired number of qualified participants.

Considering the polarizing and often multifaceted nature of voter perceptions and the decision-making process, the initial search for suitable participants focused on social media like LinkedIn, Facebook, and Twitter, where a call for participation was posted. The criterion for participation was adults who voted in government elections since 2016. Data collection for this study was conducted via Google Forms and subsequently analyzed concerning the research questions and hypotheses. Online surveys provide numerous advantages compared to in-person or mail-based questionnaires. These advantages are increased convenience and better privacy protection for participants. Furthermore, researchers also benefit from decentralized data gathering, simplified data management, and accelerated administration (Keusch, 2015).

This research employed descriptive and inferential statistics, allowing for outcome predictions through parametric methods like z-test, t-test, f-test, ANOVA, and non-parametric methods such as Chi-square (Huang, 2018; Plonsky & Oswald, 2017). To ensure accurate inferential statistical analysis, it is essential to avoid violating their assumptions (Bobak et al., 2018). Otherwise, the results may exhibit biased relationship estimates and standard errors (Schmidt & Finan, 2018). In comparison, descriptive statistics are useful for describing data by analyzing central tendencies, distribution shapes, and variability (Y. Kim et al., 2017). Unlike inferential statistics, they do not permit researchers to draw inferences.

Before examining the connections between the study variables, the data were evaluated for multicollinearity, outliers, homoscedasticity, linearity, and normality to confirm no assumption violations. Normality assumes that the population from which the data is drawn is normally distributed (Ahmad & Khan Sherwani, 2015). This study utilized a probability–probability (P-P) plot for graphical examination and normality testing (see Appendix C). P-P plots compare two data sets, a sample data set, and a normally distributed theoretical set, to ensure data points align along a straight line, indicating a suitable distribution model (Yang et al., 2017). The Shapiro-Wilk test was also employed to support the visual assessment and evaluate normality.

Homoscedasticity pertains to the equality of variances for dependent variables across all analyzed data (Pal & Lin, 2017). Linearity assumes that the relationship between independent and dependent variables is linear, represented graphically by a straight line (Kumar, 2011). Scatter plots are often utilized to test these assumptions (Rensink, 2017), and this study used these plots for visual data examination. Outliers are data points within a sample that significantly deviate from other observations (Altman & Krzywinski, 2016). They may result from sample variation or data collection errors. Researchers must clearly label and justify any ignored outliers or expand the research scope to explain their presence (Altman & Krzywinski, 2016).

Multicollinearity arises when sampled data analysis reveals high linear dependency among covariates in a regression model

(Huang et al., 2016). Researchers can test for multicollinearity through correlation analysis and by reviewing the variance inflation factor (VIF), where values greater than 10 indicate poor estimation of the corresponding ordinary least squares (OLS) coefficient parameter (CoŞKuntuncel, 2018). Although bivariate correlations exceeding .90 between predictor variables may suggest multicollinearity, researchers should consider sample size and influential factors when making determinations (R. S. Kim et al., 2017). This study tested data for multicollinearity, aiming for bivariate correlations of .90 or lower to confirm no assumption violation.

After testing for assumption violations, the Kruskal-Wallis H test, the chi-square test for independence, and Spearman's rho statistical analysis techniques were employed to evaluate the data. Statistical analyses help predict how multiple independent variables may influence a dependent variable's variation (Green & Salkind, 2016). Furthermore, the one-sample chi-square test assessed the distribution of answers concerning their expected frequencies (Miller & Salkind, 2002). These statistical analyses were suitable for this study and appropriate for examining the relationship between study variables (Hashim et al., 2018; Plonsky & Oswald, 2017).

Statistical analysis was conducted using SPSS software version 28, a popular choice among researchers due to its user-friendly interface, short learning curve, and comprehensive analysis capabilities (Green & Salkind, 2016). Dedicated statistical software solutions enable researchers to perform statistical analyses without programming or extensive computer knowledge (Bolarinwa, 2015). Additionally, the recently introduced missing values module in SPSS allows users to identify missing values post-analysis and assists with making appropriate corrections (Hutcheson & Williams, 2016).

Assumptions

Researchers' assumptions stem from their understanding and perception of reality, which inform their interpretation of the world (Haegele & Hodge, 2015). In this study, the assumption was made that quantitative methodology is appropriate, given the study's requirements. Furthermore, it was also assumed that the research design was appropriate, and that the data collection instrument was reliable and valid. Moreover, it was assumed that the data collection process was bias-free and captured the demographics of the real population of the study. Quantitative research emphasizes examining and deciphering real-world occurrences through the lens of data, sample selection, parameter approximation, model creation, equalization, theories, and hypothesis formulation (Zyphur & Pierides, 2017).

While the depiction of a global phenomenon might be realistic, accurate, and assumption-free, it is essential to remember that any conclusion drawn is, by definition, merely a highly likely match (Zyphur & Pierides, 2017). To address these assumptions, the investigator avoided direct interaction with the sample, concentrating instead on developing an impartial method to examine the relationship between the independent and dependent variables.

An additional presupposition for this investigation was that all participants felt they had been influenced by cyber-meddling to some degree and had participated in a government election since 2016. Moreover, the study assumed that the sample size was sufficient and represented the larger population accurately. It was also presumed that each participant responded to the survey queries honestly and to the best of their ability. Finally, it was assumed that the survey tool was appropriate for the study and that the quantitative research methodology facilitated gathering enough raw data to assess and answer the research questions using the selected data analysis method.

Limitations

All assumptions in this study are also its limitations. Furthermore, obstacles or potential vulnerabilities inherent in a study could incorporate matters related to behavioral, societal, relational, and causative factors, research design, external validity, and the survey tool (Schafer Astroth, 2018). For instance, the reliance on a nonexperimental research design confines this study's conclusions to the examination of the robustness of connections between the variables under study (Park & Park, 2016). Moreover, other behavioral, societal, relational, or causative elements could sway the voter decision-making process. The research tool was not crafted to accumulate data outside the scope of information presumed to be beneficial in addressing the research question. Recognizing these shortcomings minimized bias, and the data and conclusions were interpreted honestly and impartially.

Another constraint of this study was the selection of research methodology. Even though quantitative designs are sufficiently equipped to gather and evaluate empirical data, they cannot typically incorporate contextual or additional information

(Zyphur & Pierides, 2017). Hence, the findings could be restricted by the design of the survey and the chosen research methodology, although the acquired data should offer meaningful insights for prospective studies. Besides, researchers employ correlational studies to explore the interplay between dependent and independent variables, but the same approach falls short of establishing a cause-effect relationship (Kumar, 2011). Consequently, one of the study's limitations was its inability to confirm causation.

Delimitations

The study's parameters and limits, often called delimitations, were defined by its scope and boundaries (Thomas et al., 2015). Even though the study's population was drawn from various global locations, it primarily focused on recent government elections and voter beliefs. More specifically, the study boundaries were drawn around conducting research among voters who believed in having been impacted by cyber-meddling. The aim was to comprehend the relationship between perceived cyber-meddling and the voter decision-making process. By opting for a quantitative research design, the study's extent was confined to measurable data, which does not encompass the rich, descriptive details commonly found in qualitative research.

Ethical Assurances

Quantitative research methodology seeks to narrow down research queries, study variables, and test hypotheses by collecting numeric data in a highly structured setting (Rutberg & Bouikidis, 2018). This particular strategy positions the researcher as a neutral data collector, starkly contrasting with the qualitative research techniques where the investigator is essentially the primary instrument for data collection (Rutberg & Bouikidis, 2018). While there is a risk of bias in quantitative research, it can be minimized by employing tools closely related to the research theme and using a theoretical framework as the study's foundation (Zyphur & Pierides, 2017). In addition, ethical research standards can be maintained, and participant rights can be upheld by acquiring informed consent (Lühnen et al., 2018). Before participating in this study, all participants received information regarding consent (see Appendix B). They were also informed about the purpose and characteristics of the study, with assurances of confidentiality. Including these components in informed consent is a standard practice in research activities (Sugiura et al., 2016).

Summary

This research employed a quantitative methodology with a correlational, non-experimental, and cross-sectional design to explore the interconnections among the study variables. The study focused on voter beliefs and decision-making processes regarding perceived cyber interference during elections. Only participants who voted in a government election since 2016 were included in this study.

The research aimed to involve between 67 and 115 participants, as suggested by the G*Power software, to maintain a power range from .80 to .95. The data was gathered using a specially curated survey, and a preliminary study was executed to confirm the survey's validity. The survey included demographic inquiries and eleven additional questions related to the outcome predictor variable about the voter decision-making process. These questions were rated on a 5-point Likert scale, ranging from 1 (strongly disagree) to 5 (strongly agree).

Participants were approached via email or direct messaging, and data was collected through an online survey on Google Forms. To confirm no deviations from the assumptions, the variables' relationships were scrutinized for multicollinearity, outliers, homoscedasticity, linearity, and normality. SPSS software Version 28 was employed for data evaluation using the multiple regression statistical analysis technique. The developed tool's consistency was cross-checked by calculating Cronbach's α to ensure reliability and external validity was enhanced by exceeding the minimum required participant count. This section also discussed assumptions and limitations, such as the assumption that the research design was appropriate, that the data collection instrument was reliable and valid, and that the data collection process was bias-free and captured the demographics of the real population of the study. Furthermore, delimitations related to measurable data, which did not encompass the rich, descriptive details commonly found in qualitative research, as well as ethical considerations related to confidentiality and participation that shaped the research design, methodology, and execution of the study.

Chapter 4:
Findings

The purpose of this quantitative, non-experimental correlational study was to provide an understanding of the relationship between voters' belief in cyber election meddling by foreign governments and their belief on its impact on their decision-making process in government elections. This chapter's ensuing segments delve into the collected data's validity and reliability. This section further broadens to encompass a discourse on the checks for breach of assumptions; an elaboration of the findings, accentuating the spread of responses in correlation to their theoretical probabilities via the employment of the singular-sample chi-square examination, is also incorporated. Moreover, the strength of interrelationships within the data was examined using Spearman's rho statistical methodology (Miller & Salkind, 2002). Furthermore, this chapter includes a section evaluating the findings and concludes with a succinct summary.

Validity and Reliability of the Data

A self-administered survey was crafted following a preliminary investigation and evaluated by an expert panel before data gathering for the current research (Appendix A). Accuracy and credibility form the fundamental pillars of any study. Reliability lies in the precision of data collection and its capacity to yield uniform results over time (Flower et al., 2015). An instrument's reliability can be ensured by utilizing one previously successful in similar research or by evaluating its comparability, stability, and uniformity (Heale & Twycross, 2015). Although multiple methods exist to ascertain a tool's reliability, such as a test-retest sequence, measuring Cronbach's α to determine internal consistency is commonly the preferred method among researchers (Leung, 2011). As this research was based on a novel instrument, the option to consider the reliability assessments of other instruments was not available.

It is common in research to evaluate the internal consistency or homogeneity of a survey tool through methods such as correlation between items, split-half reliability, or Cronbach's α (Heale & Twycross, 2015). In this specific investigation, Cronbach's α was the chosen method to confirm the reliability of the employed instrument. Cronbach's α calculates the average of all correlations in every possible combination using split halves, resulting in a value ranging from 0 to 1. A score of 0.7 or above generally signifies acceptable reliability (Heale & Twycross, 2015; López et al., 2018). This survey included 11 non-demographic queries, all based on a 5-point Likert scale ranging from "strongly disagree" to "strongly agree," and all achieved a Cronbach's α exceeding .70 (Table 1). This suggests that the data collected from the questions in this study is satisfactorily reliable.

Table 1.
Reliability Statistics

Cronbach's Alpha	Cronbach's Alpha Based on Standardized Items	Number of Non-Demographic Survey Questions
.721	.752	11

Evaluating the accuracy of a research tool, especially in surveys, is crucial. This accuracy, known as validity, is tied to the degree to which the tool can successfully measure a desired variable (Bolarinwa, 2015). Validity comes in multiple forms, such as internal and external validity, face validity, construct validity, content validity, and criterion validity, among others (Heale & Twycross, 2015).

Internal validity is achieved when there is a provable causal link between the studied variables, meaning that the data collected convincingly demonstrates one variable's impact on another (Torre & Picho, 2016). The assessment of internal validity is a common practice in experimental designs as it helps confirm causal relationships. Nevertheless, there exists a potential threat that the changes observed are due to unidentified intermediary factors rather than the effect of study variables on each other (Bernstein, 2018). Researchers depend on criterion validity to assess the causal connection between the items on a survey and their reflection of actual conditions in the world (Bolarinwa, 2015). Since the objective of this study was not to determine causality but to uncover the magnitude of the relationships between voters' belief in cyber election meddling by foreign governments and their belief in its impact on their decision-making process in government, the internal validity of the tool was not a point of focus.

External validity pertains to the degree to which the outcomes of a study and the data collected can be generalized to a broader population (Torre & Picho, 2016). A significant element influencing external validity is the transferability and size of the sample (Bernstein, 2018). By increasing the number of study participants, researchers can enhance external validity as the sample becomes more reflective of the population, thereby boosting the likelihood of accurate parameter approximation (Zyphur & Pierides, 2017). Also, researchers can boost external validity by adhering to suitable sampling methods, minimizing sampling bias and error, and choosing a representative sample (Hales, 2016). A minimum of 67 participants was the estimated appropriate sample size for this study. The data gathering concluded with 124 eligible participants, exceeding the estimated minimum, which implies a higher-than-average external validity for this investigation.

Although P-P plots visually suggested that the data gathered in this research is largely normalized, the subsequent Shapiro-Wilk test did not corroborate this. If the data had shown normal distribution, it would have facilitated the use of various statistical methods such as multiple linear regression, hypothesis testing, and Pearson's r. However, given the non-parametric nature of the data, a different approach was necessary. Consequently, a one-sample chi-square test was employed to assess the observed frequency of data against the expected distribution. On the other hand, Spearman's rho was used to determine the correlations between variables. Additionally, the chi-square test of independence and the Kruskal-Wallis H were calculated to enhance the statistical analysis results.

Results

Using the developed and validated questionnaire, the following data collection efforts resulted in 124 recorded responses. Only the completed survey results were counted. At the end of the data collection, all responses were exported as a CSV file and then imported into SPSS Version 28 for further analysis. Because only complete responses were included in the data export and following analysis, all data considered for this research are valid. From within this final dataset, all respondents disclosed their gender.

Even though potential participants were contacted regardless of their gender, the majority of participants were male (60.5%) (Table 2). Participants also aged above and below 60 years old, with 67.7% stating an age below 51. Furthermore, 32.2% of participants stated they were 51 years or older. In particular, the age of participants was similarly distributed between 31 and 60 years, suggesting various levels of work experience and seniority. Additionally, most participants had a Bachelor's degree or lower qualification, with Master's or Doctorate holders making up 45.1% of the participants. It needs to be noted that participants with tertiary education may have a better understanding and awareness of the issues this research tried to assess.

Table 2.

Gender Distribution Across the Sample

	Frequency	Percent	Valid Percent	Cumulative Percent
Female	49	39.5	39.5	39.5

I do not wish to disclose	0	0	0	0
Male	75	60.5	60.5	60.5
Total	124	100.0	100.0	100.0

Most participants identified as Caucasian/White (54.8%); 8.9% identified as African American, 9.7% as Asian, and 11.3% as Hispanic, with other races accounting for the rest of the participants. Most participants (67.7%) identified North America as the region in which they voted most recently. Western Europe (15.3%) and Eastern Europe (11.3%) were also selected, with Africa, Asia, and South America accounting for the remainder. Although 54.8% of participants identified as Caucasian/White, the most recent census estimate suggested that White Americans make up 75.5% of the population in the US (United States Census Bureau, 2022). Considering the diversity of ethnic groups in Western and Eastern Europe and their smaller contribution to the population in this study, the participant pool seems biased toward diversity, which does not align with the respective distribution of races, at least within the US.

Participants also relied on traditional media for information about candidates and parties during elections. While most participants selected a combination of news sources, some individual sources stood out; sixteen participants (21%) suggested that cable news is their only source of information regarding elections and candidates. In stark contrast, 16 (12.9%) participants suggested that they do not rely on any traditional media to inform their decisions. Furthermore, nine (7.3%) participants declared that they only use newspapers as their source of information. While the reliance on traditional media may suggest a more balanced exposure to news, especially in the

US, social media and traditional media are highly unbalanced and partisan (Benkler et al., 2018). However, it must be noted that the data in this study suggests that a general preference for using social media as a news source is prevalent across all participants and not just limited to those from the US.

When participants noted using social media to gather information about candidates and elections, 78 participants mentioned Facebook (Meta). However, only two (1.6%) participants suggested that Facebook is their only source of news, whereas 79 (63.7%) said that Facebook is just a part of the sources they rely on. Most participants suggested using Facebook with other social media services like LinkedIn, Reddit, Instagram, TikTok, or Twitter. However, ten (8.1%) participants declared they do not use mainstream social media services but instead rely on other sources. Here, it becomes evident that most participants in this study must have been exposed to election interference attempts on social media, regardless of whether they perceived it as such. With documented social media cyber meddling in most recent elections, it is conceivable that most participants have been influenced by these attempts to sway voter perception.

One-sample chi-square test. The one-sample chi-square test was employed to analyze the responses' dispersion according to their corresponding anticipated frequencies (Miller & Salkind, 2002). An argument can be made that data gathered via a Likert scale may demonstrate a greater propensity to vary from the theoretical distributions that the Chi-Square test assigns to each potential response. However, even though a Likert scale is inherently ordinal, its even spacing and directionality make it suitable for interpretation through an interval scale instead (Chyung et al., 2017; Leung, 2011). Therefore, it could still indicate the response trends, inferring a more potent or less potent than a relative distribution of the responses (Green & Salkind, 2016). All non-demographic inquiries (Q1-Q11) underwent a one-sample chi-square examination. The consolidated findings for all questions are illustrated in Table 3. While most questions exhibited higher levels of concurrence than discord, several results were notably prominent. Specifically, the responses to Q4, Q6, and Q7 demonstrated an overwhelming consensus of more than 79% among the respondents.

The results of the one-sample chi-square test for assessing participant agreement with whether they believe what is presented in non-traditional media like social media or blog posts about political candidates and their programs in government elections since 2016 can be misleading (Q4) was significant, $\chi^2(4, N = 124) = 101.24$, $p < .01$. The proportion of participants who strongly agreed, or agreed with this statement ($p = .81$) was much greater than the hypothesized proportion of .40. Overall, these results signify that the majority of the participants believe that non-traditional media like social media or blog posts about political candidates and their programs in government elections since 2016 can be misleading.

Table 3.
One-Sample Chi-Square Test Results

	Q1	Q2	Q3	Q4	Q5	Q6	Q7	Q8	Q9	Q10	Q11
Chi-Squa re	59.87 1[a]	12.129 [a]	79.629[a]	101.242[a]	67.855[a]	99.629[a]	103.742[a]	32.855[a]	36.242[a]	84.306[a]	42.129[a]
df	4	4	4	4	4	4	4	4	4	4	4

Asymp. Sig.	0.000	0.016	0.000	0.000	0.000	0.000	0.000	0.000	0.000	0.000	0.000

a. 0 cells (0.0%) have expected frequencies less than 5. The minimum expected cell frequency is 24.8.

Similarly, the results of the one-sample chi-square test for assessing participant agreement with whether they believe there was cyber election meddling by foreign governments since 2016 through non-traditional media like social media or blog posts (Q6) was significant, $\chi^2(4, N = 124) = 99.63$, $p < .01$. The proportion of participants who strongly agreed or agreed with this statement ($p = .79$) was much greater than the hypothesized proportion of .40. Overall, these results demonstrate that the majority of the participants believe that there was cyber election meddling by foreign governments since 2016 through non-traditional media like social media or blog posts.

Moreover, the results of the one-sample chi-square test for assessing participant agreement with whether they believe cyber election meddling by foreign governments since 2016 affected the voting procedures and processes (Q7) was also significant, $\chi^2(4, N = 124) = 103.74$, $p < .01$. The proportion of participants who strongly agreed or agreed with this statement ($p = .79$) was much greater than the hypothesized proportion of .40. Overall, these results imply that the overwhelming majority of participants believe cyber election meddling by foreign governments since 2016 affected the voting procedures and processes.

It needs to be noted that this observation is somewhat at odds with the participants' views on how meddling influenced their perception. Here, the results of the one-sample chi-square test for assessing participant agreement with whether they believe cyber election meddling by foreign governments might have influenced their perception of political candidates and their programs in government elections since 2016 (Q8) was not significant, $\chi^2(4, N = 124) = 32.86, p < .01$. The proportion of participants who strongly disagreed or disagreed with this statement ($p = .36$) was greater than those who agreed or strongly agreed with this statement. However, a large proportion ($p = .28$) could not agree or disagree with this statement, especially because participants agreed that cyber election meddling took place in recent elections and these attempts actively influenced the election processes, seeing participants reject the notion that their perception was influenced seems at odds with the previous statements.

Participants also seemed to agree with Q1, Q3, and Q10, although the strength of agreement was weaker than with Q4, Q6, and Q7. The results of the one-sample chi-square test for assessing participant agreement with whether they rely on traditional media such as cable, radio, or newspapers to get their information about political candidates and their programs in government elections since 2016 (Q1) was significant, $\chi^2(4, N = 124) = 59.87, p < .01$. The proportion of participants who strongly agreed or agreed with this statement ($p = .66$) was much greater than the hypothesized proportion of .40. Overall, these results show that the majority of the participants rely on traditional media such as cable, radio, or newspapers to get their information about political candidates and their programs in government elections since 2016.

Similarly, the results of the one-sample chi-square test for assessing participant agreement with whether they believe what is presented in traditional media like cable, radio, or newspapers about political candidates and their programs in government elections since 2016 can be misleading (Q3) was significant, $\chi^2(4, N = 124) = 79.63, p < .01$. The proportion of participants who strongly agreed or agreed with this statement ($p = .64$) was much greater than the hypothesized proportion of .40. Overall, these results indicate that the majority of the participants believe what is presented in traditional media like cable, radio, or newspapers about political candidates and their programs in government elections since 2016 can be misleading.

Lastly, the results of the one-sample chi-square test for assessing participant agreement with whether they believe cyber election meddling by foreign governments has resulted in unfair processes in government elections since 2016 (Q10) was significant, $\chi^2(4, N = 124) = 84.31, p < .01$. The proportion of participants who strongly agreed or agreed with this statement ($p = .62$) was much greater than the hypothesized proportion of .40 suggesting that the majority of the participants believe cyber election meddling by foreign governments has resulted in unfair processes in government elections since 2016.

Spearman's rho test. Spearman's rho correlation coefficient was used to evaluate the strength of the relationships between the non-demographic questions. Several correlations stood out, especially on the more significant $p < .01$ level, including correlations between Q4 and Q9, Q4 and Q11, and Q7 and Q9 (Table 4). In particular, there was a significant correlation between the belief that what is presented in non-traditional media, like social media or blog posts about political candidates and their programs in government elections since 2016 can be misleading (Q4) and the belief that cyber election meddling by foreign governments might have influenced the participant's decision-making process in government elections since 2016 (Q9), r_s=.23, p=.01, N=124. As such, most participants seemed to agree that cyber meddling on social media has influenced the participant's decision-making process in government elections.

Similarly, Spearman's rho coefficient was used to assess the relationship between the belief that what is presented in non-traditional media, like social media or blog posts about political candidates and their programs in government elections since 2016 can be misleading (Q4) and the belief that cyber election meddling by foreign governments has resulted in governments that do not represent the people (Q11). There was a significant correlation between the two, r_s=.22, p=.01, N=124. Interestingly, this correlation may suggest that cyber-meddling campaigns on social media may have successfully elected governments that are not representative of the people, even though this study did not assess the extent or direction of this perceived misrepresentation. Therefore, it seems most participants were unhappy about the outcomes of recent elections and how they represent the people.

Table 4.

Spearman's Rho for Non-Demographic Questions

		Q1	Q2	Q3	Q4	Q5	Q6	Q7	Q8	Q9	Q10	Q11
Q1	Correlation Coefficient	1.000	-.283**	-0.158	0.174	-0.043	0.165	.199*	0.078	0.048	0.109	0.043
	Sig. (2-tailed)		0.001	0.080	0.053	0.634	0.066	0.027	0.392	0.594	0.230	0.634
	N	124	124	124	124	124	124	124	124	124	124	124

70

Q2	Correlation Coefficient	1.000	.365**	-.179*	0.140	-.205*	-0.067	.188*	.189*	0.041	-0.040
	Sig. (2-tailed)		0.000	0.046	0.121	0.023	0.461	0.037	0.036	0.653	0.663
	N	124	124	124	124	124	124	124	124	124	124
Q3	Correlation Coefficient		1.000	0.072	.473**	-0.064	0.125	0.105	0.117	0.050	0.002
	Sig. (2-tailed)			0.426	0.000	0.481	0.165	0.247	0.196	0.580	0.980
	N		124	124	124	124	124	124	124	124	124
Q4	Correlation Coefficient			1.000	0.150	.568**	.394**	0.108	.229*	.368**	.224*
	Sig. (2-tailed)				0.096	0.000	0.000	0.231	0.010	0.000	0.012
	N			124	124	124	124	124	124	124	124
Q5	Correlation Coefficient				1.000	.306**	.275**	.212*	0.147	.303**	.301**
	Sig. (2-tailed)					0.001	0.002	0.018	0.103	0.001	0.001
	N				124	124	124	124	124	124	124
Q6	Correlation Coefficient					1.000	.488**	0.120	0.130	.419**	.319**
	Sig. (2-tailed)						0.000	0.184	0.150	0.000	0.000
	N					124	124	124	124	124	124
Q7	Correlation Coefficient						1.000	.210*	.224*	.593**	.255**

	Sig. (2-tailed)				0.019	0.013	0.000	0.004
	N		124	124	124	124	124
Q8	Correlation Coefficient			1.000	.786**	.191*	.256**
	Sig. (2-tailed)				0.000	0.034	0.004
	N			124	124	124	124
Q9	Correlation Coefficient				1.000	0.143	0.137
	Sig. (2-tailed)					0.114	0.129
	N				124	124	124
Q10	Correlation Coefficient					1.000	.411**
	Sig. (2-tailed)						0.000
	N					124	124
Q11	Correlation Coefficient						1.000
	Sig. (2-tailed)						
	N						124

**. Correlation is significant at the 0.01 level (2-tailed).

*. Correlation is significant at the 0.05 level (2-tailed).

Furthermore, a significant correlation between the belief that there was cyber election meddling by foreign governments since

2016 through non-traditional media like social media or blog posts (Q7) and the belief that cyber election meddling by foreign governments might have influenced the participant's decision-making process in government elections since 2016 (Q9) was also evident with r_s=.22, p=.01, N=124. Spearman's rho further indicated a relationship at the $p < .05$ level between whether participants relied on traditional media such as cable, radio, or newspapers as the source for information about political candidates and their programs in government elections since 2016 (Q1) and the belief that there was cyber election meddling by foreign governments since 2016 through non-traditional media like social media or blog posts (Q7), with r_s=.2, p=.03, N=124.

Another significant relationship emerged between the reliance on non-traditional media, such as social network sites or blog posts for information about political candidates and their programs in government elections since 2016 (Q2) and the belief that what is presented in non-traditional media like social media or blog posts about political candidates and their programs in government elections since 2016 can be misleading (Q4), r_s=-.18, p=.05, N=124. Surprisingly, participants who relied on social media for information about political candidates also believed that this information regarding government elections could be misleading, suggesting that even though participants use social media as a source of information, they also questioned its trustworthiness.

Spearman's rho also indicated a significant correlation between the reliance on non-traditional media, such as social network sites or blog posts, for information about political candidates and their programs in government elections since 2016 (Q2) and the belief that there was cyber election meddling by foreign governments since 2016 through non-traditional media like social media or blog posts (Q6), r_s=-.20, p=.02, N=124. Spearman's rho also indicated a significant correlation between Q2 and the belief that cyber election meddling by foreign governments might have influenced my perception of political candidates and their programs in government elections since 2016 (Q8), r_s=.19, p=.04, N=124. Lastly, Q2 also significantly correlated with the belief that cyber election meddling by foreign governments might have influenced my decision-making process in government elections since 2016 (Q9), r_s=.19, p=.04, N=124. Participants in this study seem to suggest that they are aware of cyber-meddling on social media, believe they have been exposed to these efforts, and, as a result, that their decision-making process may have been influenced. Considering that in some instances, seven years may have passed since participants were exposed to cyber meddling during the 2016 presidential election in the US, the study's instrument did not assess whether participants were aware of these influence campaigns back then or whether this is a newfound understanding that only recently developed.

In line with these findings, the belief that there has been cyber election meddling by foreign governments since 2016 through traditional media like cable, radio, or newspapers (Q5) and the belief that cyber election meddling by foreign governments might have influenced the voter's perception about political candidates and their programs in government elections since 2016 (Q8) also showed a strong interrelationship with

r_s=.21, p=.02, N=124. Spearman's rho also indicated significant correlations between the belief that cyber election meddling by foreign governments since 2016 affected the voting procedures and processes (Q7) and Q8 (r_s=.21, p=.02, N=124), as well as Q7 and the belief that cyber election meddling by foreign governments might have influenced the voter's perception about political candidates and their programs in government elections since 2016Q9 (r_s=.22, p=.01, N=124). Lastly, a connection also existed between the belief that cyber election meddling by foreign governments might have influenced the voter's perception of political candidates and their programs in government elections since 2016 (Q8) and the belief that cyber election meddling by foreign governments has resulted in unfair processes in government elections since 2016 (Q10) (r_s=.19, p=.03, N=124). Participants here seem to suggest that they believe that cyber-meddling took place across all forms of media and that these misinformation campaigns profoundly impacted government elections and voter perceptions.

Chi-Square test for independence. A Chi-Square test for independence was executed on all non-demographic questions (refer to Appendix D). The chi-square test for independence is frequently utilized by researchers on non-parametric data to scrutinize variances between groups and assess if variables operate independently (McHugh, 2013). The findings from the chi-square test of independence unveiled a substantial dependence at or around the p=.05 level amidst the majority of the questions. These dependencies frequently coincide with the correlations previously identified via Spearman's rho, albeit with several discrepancies.

Moreover, several potent associations below the p=.01 level are notably present. For example, a strong association was found between the use of traditional media as an election information resource (Q1) and the use of non-traditional media, such as social media (Q2), $\chi^2(16)> = 36.475$, $p = .002$, Q1 and the belief that cyber election meddling by foreign governments might have influenced the voter's perception about political candidates and their programs in government elections since 2016 (Q8), $\chi^2(16)> = 35.787$, $p = .003$), and Q1 and the belief that cyber election meddling by foreign governments might have influenced the voter's decision-making process in government elections since 2016 (Q9) ($\chi^2(16)> = 39.398$, $p = .001$).

Spearman's Rho identified similar relationships, further emphasizing how most participants believe that election interference took place and that it was not limited to social media or blog posts alone but rather widespread across all forms of media. Surprisingly, although a strong relationship between Q1 and Q2 exists, the observed relationships between Q1 and Q8 and Q1 and Q9 only partially translate to the relationships between Q2 and Q8 and Q2 and Q9. Q2 and Q9 did not exhibit a strong relationship. In contrast, Q2 and Q8 showed a strong interconnection with $\chi2(16)> = 30.699$, p = .015); however, this connection is arguably weaker than the one observed between Q1 and Q8. Except for the relationships between Q1 and Q6 and Q7, Q2 and Q7, Q2 and Q9 and Q10, Q3 and Q8, Q4 and Q8 and Q9, and Q6 and Q8, all other pairings showed strong relationships below the *p*=.05 level.

Kruskal-Wallis H test. The Kruskal-Wallis H test was computed between important demographic questions and all non-demographic questions (Table 5). The analysis of variance (ANOVA) is a common tool employed by investigators to identify statistical discrepancies between the means of two groups, interventions, or change metrics (Green & Salkind, 2016). However, it is worth noting that the prerequisite for a one-way ANOVA evaluation is that the data should follow a normal distribution. This research treated the data as non-parametric, thus justifying using the Kruskal-Wallis H test as a more suitable method. The findings from the Kruskal-Wallis evaluation were largely decisive, revealing substantial disparities in the means across most items scrutinized. Some outcomes were particularly noteworthy.

Table 5.
Kruskal-Wallis H Test Between Important Demographic Questions and Q1 to Q11

Group		Q1	Q2	Q3	Q4	Q5	Q6	Q7	Q8	Q9	Q10	Q11
What is your race?	Kruskal-Wallis H	12.210	14.470	3.236	15.453	16.225	12.887	23.838	6.787	6.791	18.449	8.479
	df	12	12	12	12	12	12	12	12	12	12	12
	Asymp. Sig.	0.429	0.272	0.994	0.218	0.181	0.377	0.021	0.871	0.871	0.103	0.747
In which region did you most recently cast your vote in a	Kruskal-Wallis H	5.551	20.192	4.843	8.889	5.919	7.288	6.619	5.105	4.213	11.060	7.079
	df	5	5	5	5	5	5	5	5	5	5	5
	Asymp. Sig.	0.352	0.001	0.435	0.114	0.314	0.200	0.251	0.403	0.519	0.050	0.215

governmental election?												
What is your highest level of education?	Kruskal-Wallis H	6.499	6.364	12.903	18.020	9.617	15.295	12.533	16.106	12.700	8.981	6.750
	df	8	8	8	8	8	8	8	8	8	8	8
	Asymp. Sig.	0.591	0.607	0.115	0.021	0.293	0.054	0.129	0.041	0.123	0.344	0.564
What is your age?	Kruskal-Wallis H	10.056	31.996	9.714	2.957	7.963	10.184	4.046	3.101	3.818	1.350	3.861
	df	4	4	4	4	4	4	4	4	4	4	4
	Asymp. Sig.	0.039	0.000	0.046	0.565	0.093	0.037	0.400	0.541	0.431	0.853	0.425
What is your gender?	Kruskal-Wallis H	0.791	2.423	1.250	0.104	0.066	0.197	3.378	0.235	0.051	3.493	0.276
	df	1	1	1	1	1	1	1	1	1	1	1
	Asymp. Sig.	0.374	0.120	0.264	0.447	0.797	0.657	0.066	0.628	0.821	0.062	0.599

For example, in the groupings between the demographic questions and the belief that cyber election meddling by foreign governments since 2016 affected the voting procedures and processes (Q7), race stood out with $\chi^2(12) = 23.838, p = .021$. In contrast, connections between the region in which the participants most recently cast their vote in a governmental election and the reliance on non-traditional media such as social network sites or blog posts for information about political candidates and their programs in government elections since 2016 (Q2), $\chi^2(55) = 20.192$, $p = .001$, as well as the belief that cyber election meddling by foreign governments has resulted in unfair processes in government elections since 2016 (Q10) with $\chi^2(5) = 11.060$, $p = .05$) existed. With a diverse, non-homogenous participant pool, the racial distribution and use of various media sources should be expected to vary, especially because voters in North America and Europe have been exposed to different misinformation campaigns and different degrees.

Additional relationships existed between the highest level of education and the belief that what is presented in non-traditional media, like social media or blog posts about political candidates and their programs in government elections since 2016, can be misleading (Q4), $\chi^2(8) = 18.020$, $p = .021$, and the belief that there was cyber election meddling by foreign governments since 2016 through non-traditional media like social media or blog posts (Q6), $\chi^2(8) = 15.295$, $p = .054$. Furthermore, the education level is also strongly related to the belief that cyber election meddling by foreign governments might have influenced voters' perception of political candidates and their programs in government elections since 2016 with $\chi^2(8) = 16.106$, $p = .041$. This observation aligns with other observations in this study, where those participants who are better educated and informed are more likely to identify misinformation campaigns and how they may impact the voter decision-making process.

Lastly, age was significantly related to how participants answered Q1, Q2, Q3 and Q6. Respectively, these interrelationships included $\chi^2(4) = 10.056$, $p = .039$ (Q1), $\chi^2(4) =$

31.996, $p = .0$ (Q2), $\chi^2(4) = 9.714$, $p = .046$ (Q3), and $\chi^2(4) = 10.184$, $p = .037$ (Q6). While the Kruskal-Wallis H test did not indicate significant differences for most subject matter questions in relation to demographics, the results suggest that participants answered a few questions differently based on their race, age, the region in which they voted, and their level of education. Some of these relationships may indicate that the impact of perceived cyber election meddling varies across jurisdictions, levels of education, or age.

Research Questions and Hypotheses

Concerning the research question and associated hypothesis about the relationship between voters' belief in cyber election meddling by foreign governments and their belief in its impact on their decision-making process in government elections, 81% of all participants believed that what is presented in non-traditional media, like social media or blog posts about political candidates and their programs in government elections since 2016 can be misleading (Q4). Similarly, 80% of participants believed that there was cyber election meddling by foreign governments since 2016 through non-traditional media like social media or blog posts, and 79% believed that cyber election meddling by foreign governments since 2016 affected the voting procedures and processes. Furthermore, Spearman's Rho and the chi-square test of independence identified several strong relationships between statements related to cyber meddling and the belief that these actions have influenced the participant's perception of political candidates and their decision-making process during government elections since 2016. Therefore, the null hypothesis H0 was rejected. The results confirmed a relationship between voters' belief in cyber election meddling by foreign governments and their belief on its impact on their decision-making process in government.

Evaluation of the Findings

While some of the research participants in Europe have likely been exposed to cyber meddling (Bollmann & Gibeon, 2022; Cadwalladr & Graham-Harrison, 2018; Downing & Ahmed, 2019; Ellehuus & Ruy, 2020), the majority of the documented interference is related to the US (Cahill, 2017; Jarvis, 2018; Sander, 2019). Thus, with most of the participants having voted in North America, it is conceivable that they must have been exposed to cyber meddling during one or more recent elections in that region. Similar to other research that suggested that voters who rely on various sources of information about candidates and elections are better equipped to make informed decisions (Alashri et al., 2016; Mercier et al., 2017), participants in this study were also more likely to believe that election interference took place through social media when they relied on information sources other than blog posts or social media alone.

Moreover, in line with what some researchers observed in other studies related to self-regulation (Schunk & Usher, 2019; Zimmerman & Schunk, 2004), participants seemed more likely to assume that others have been impacted while they managed to avoid being influenced, even if they failed to admit that their decision-making process may have been compromised as well. This observation aligns with the tenets of the SCT, which posits that individuals acquire knowledge and skills through the interplay of personal, behavioral, and environmental factors (Bandura, 1986). As such, the process of identifying and internalizing actions is a process that is driven by social interactions and self-reflection (Bandura, 2001, 2018). Although participants in this study may have reached a level of understanding of the impact of cyber-meddling, like others, they may yet have to realize how they may have been influenced by disinformation campaigns as well (Benkler et al., 2018; Lysenko & Brooks, 2018; Schia & Gjesvik, 2020).

Furthermore, the extant literature suggests that social media can have a significant impact on the effectiveness of cyber-meddling as a tool for influencing the voter decision-making process (Agrawal, 2020; Allcott et al., 2019; Benkler et al., 2018; Downing & Ahmed, 2019; Garrett, 2019; Grinberg et al., 2019; Jalli et al., 2019; Wu et al., 2019). Although participants generally believed that cyber-meddling has occurred since 2016 and that misinformation is prevalent on traditional and non-traditional news sources, many participants were less convinced that perceived misinformation impacted their voting decision-making process. However, demographics and jurisdictions are significant factors when determining whether cyber-meddling effectively influences voters or how they perceive misinformation (Garrett, 2019; Guess et al., 2019; Sharma, 2017; Wu et al., 2022).

In line with these assumptions, participants in this study also expressed different agreements on whether social media and blog posts can be misleading depending on their level of education. Although other researchers noted that misinformation is often disguised as legitimate news and that trust can be established through social group dynamics, such as social media (Kalsnes, 2018; Sullo, 2020), most participants in this study suggested that they are aware of misinformation on these news sources. However, it was unclear whether participants were fully aware of these manipulations' extent and how they affected them. Furthermore, often those who have been subjected to influencing campaigns fail to realize that their beliefs have been impacted, and thus their decision-making process is compromised (Bradshaw & Howard, 2018; Lysenko & Brooks, 2018; Mercier et al., 2017; Schia & Gjesvik, 2020; Sharma, 2017).

Observations in this study align with the tenets of the SCT, which posits that individuals acquire knowledge and skills through the interplay of personal, behavioral, and environmental factors (Bandura, 1986). As such, the process of identifying and internalizing actions is a process that is driven by social interactions and self-reflection (Bandura, 2001, 2018). Although participants in this study may have reached a level of understanding of the impact of cyber-meddling, like others, they may yet have to realize how they may have been influenced by disinformation campaigns as well (Benkler et al., 2018; Lysenko & Brooks, 2018; Schia & Gjesvik, 2020).

Summary

This chapter delved into the robustness and dependability of the data, research outcomes, and the evaluation of the resulting findings. As the investigation was based on a newly developed instrument, reliability evaluations of pre-existing tools were not feasible. Consequently, Cronbach's alpha was calculated, which measured .721, signifying the instrument's satisfactory reliability. The study's external validity was enhanced by obtaining responses from 124 voters, significantly more than the minimum of 67. Before interpreting the results, a check for the normality of the collected data was conducted. Although p-p plots visually suggested a relatively normal data distribution, the subsequent Shapiro-Wilks test did not validate this. Hence, all subsequent statistical examinations treated the gathered data as non-parametric.

60.5% of all participants were male, 39.5% were female, and they were above and below 60 years old, with 67.7% stating an age below 51. Furthermore, 32.2% of participants stated they were 51 years or older. In particular, the age of participants was similarly distributed between 31 and 60 years, suggesting various levels of work experience and seniority. Additionally, most participants had a Bachelor's degree or lower qualification, with Master's or Doctorate holders making up 45.1% of the participants. Following the analysis of demographics, a one-sample chi-square test was used to evaluate the theoretically expected distribution of answers against the actual participant responses.

Furthermore, Spearman's rho was used to identify the strength of the relationships between the 11 non-demographic questions. Several correlations emerged, suggesting a relationship between voters' belief in cyber election meddling by foreign governments and their belief on its impact on their decision-making process in government. The chi-square independence test further affirmed these associations. Nevertheless, it is important to note that this specific test revealed several other dependencies deemed insignificant in the earlier computed Spearman's rho. This chapter concluded with an analysis of the findings, suggesting that even though there is a relationship between voters' belief in cyber election meddling by foreign governments and their belief in its impact on their decision-making process in government, the study did not assess the basis of these relationships. Lastly, some participants may not believe that misinformation has influenced their decision-making process regarding their voter preferences, even though the extant literature suggests that many misinformation campaigns have successfully changed voter perception and influenced their actions.

Chapter 5:
Implications, Recommendations, and Conclusions

The specific problem this study aimed to address was the lack of understanding among some voters regarding the relationship between their belief in cyber election meddling by foreign governments and its impact on their decision-making process in government elections (Baines & Jones, 2018; Sander, 2019). Therefore, the purpose of this quantitative, non-experimental descriptive study was to provide an understanding of the relationship between voters' belief in cyber election meddling by foreign governments and their belief in its impact on their decision-making process in government elections. The data analysis revealed several trends and correlations among specific queries within the sample population. The one-sample chi-square test indicated strong participant agreement for all the questions. Significant relationships between many queries were unveiled through Spearman's Rho. Additionally, the chi-square test for independence identified numerous dependencies among certain queries, such as those between Q1 and Q2, Q1 and Q8, and Q1 and Q9, none of which were detected by Spearman's Rho test. Furthermore, a Kruskal-Wallis H test was conducted to enrich the results section and determine if responses significantly varied across the demographic spectrum. The findings suggest that perceptions of cyber-meddling and its influence are influenced by regional location, race, education level, and age. This study, however, had several limitations. The chosen nonexperimental research design limited the analysis to only assessing the strength of the relationships between the study variables (Park & Park, 2016). Furthermore, the survey instrument was not designed to gather data beyond what was required to address the research question. Specifically, while the questionnaire aimed to explore issues related to cyber-meddling and information resources post-2016, it lacked comprehensive questions that could identify specific perceptions or the factors influencing these perceptions. The chosen research methodology also led to a deficiency in contextual information. While quantitative designs are proficient in collecting and analyzing empirical data, they typically lack the capacity to incorporate contextual or supplementary details (Zyphur & Pierides, 2017). As a result, delving into the cognitive processes underlying participants' beliefs regarding their respective responses fell outside the purview of the research design and its objectives. Lastly, owing to the utilization of a correlational methodology, the study could only investigate the relationships between the dependent and independent variables, without establishing causality (Kumar, 2011). This chapter provides an in-depth analysis of the study's implications and transitions into several practical recommendations to advance the discourse and stimulate organizational change. The study identified significant relationships and underscored disparities among participants and their beliefs about cyber-meddling and news sources, while also indicating new areas for future research. This potential for further exploration is also addressed in this section. Ultimately, the chapter focuses on concluding the study, summarizing its findings, and discussing the implications for combating cyber-meddling.

Implications

The research question in this study explored the relationships between voters' belief in cyber election meddling by foreign governments and its impact on their decision-making processes in government elections. The results of the one-sample chi-square test revealed that participants generally agreed above the theorized frequency with all questions they were asked to answer (Table 3). Additionally, the findings of Spearman's Rho supported the understanding that participants were generally aware of cyber-meddling since 2016, regardless of their primary media sources for political information (Table 4). These findings suggest that the prevailing understanding of how cyber-meddling impacts voter decision-making processes may need updating.

The extant literature indicates that voters may have been previously unaware of the impact of misinformation campaigns. However, participants in this study suggested that they are now mostly aware of these campaigns. Consequently, policies and practices cannot solely focus on identifying misinformation but must also consider whether cyber-meddling continues to influence voter decisions or if awareness of misinformation is sufficient to counter its effects. Interestingly, Spearman's Rho indicated no relationship between the majority of questions, suggesting potential additional factors regarding the voter decision-making process that this study did not assess. Furthermore, merely facilitating the labeling or identification of misinformation may not suffice to limit its spread. Policymakers should consider taking further action to mitigate its impact or its ability to spread rapidly across social and traditional media.

While the research question regarding the relationships between voters' belief in cyber election meddling by foreign governments and its impact on their decision-making process in government elections was affirmed, the research design did not establish causation. The findings support the notion that voters understand the impact of cyber-meddling on voter decision-making, although participants did not universally express that they were influenced. They suggested, however, that other voters, in general, may have been impacted. This finding raises questions about whether some participants perceive those with differing views as spreading misinformation, and vice versa. If true, participants may have difficulty discerning misinformation and could label information they disagree with as such, regardless of its validity.

Moreover, while Spearman's Rho indicated relationships between perceived cyber-meddling, its impact on elections and perceptions, and its connection to media sources, the Kruskal-Wallis H test suggested that participants responded differently based on their race, voting region, age, and educational background (Table 5). Although regional differences might be expected, notable correlations with age arose due to differing exposure to cyber-meddling efforts across regions and the influence of educational background on understanding cyber-meddling efforts. While previous research has suggested that election interference is more prevalent among younger audiences who often use social media more frequently, participants in this study also indicated that traditional media disseminated misleading information. This raises questions about whether cyber-meddling targets age groups differently through various approaches and media sources.

Recommendations for Practice

Although most participants acknowledged that cyber-meddling had influenced the voter decision-making process, they often claimed that this influence did not affect them personally. These observations may stem from recent media coverage, suggesting that cyber-meddling continues to shape voter perceptions and reactions to these influence campaigns. Media coverage of misinformation and media companies' biases may exacerbate the spread of false information. Instead, media companies should act as unbiased information gatekeepers, particularly in the US, and policies should be implemented to enforce this. While there is a risk of curtailing free speech, it is important to recognize that free speech also has its limits.

A study finding confirmed that age, jurisdiction, and level of education significantly influence voter beliefs and perceptions regarding cyber-meddling and its impact on election outcomes. While various age groups reported similar observations about cyber-meddling and its impact, these perceptions varied based on education level. Therefore, when combating cyber-meddling, considering educational levels may be more critical than previously thought. Policymakers may need to adapt their strategies for identifying misinformation and limiting its dissemination to better accommodate educational differences, as these differences can significantly shape perceptions.

Although better-educated participants generally believed that election-meddling occurred and influenced the voter decision-making process, they also indicated that they use social media and traditional media to the same extent as most other participants. Despite assuming exposure to similar cyber-meddling campaigns, some participants may simply believe they have identified misinformation and avoided its impact on their decision-making process, even though their perceptions may have been altered. Thus, merely educating voters may not suffice to help them recognize misinformation when their information sources are biased. Consequently, researchers and lawmakers should not disregard cyber-meddling as a problem associated solely with educational levels or exposure to social media. Instead, stakeholders should strive for a system where news is fact-based and clearly distinguished from opinions expressed by talk hosts or news anchors.

Recommendations for Future Research

The data in this study suggests that voters may be susceptible to cyber-meddling and misinformation campaigns regardless of the region in which they voted or the media sources they use to gather information about elections and candidates. Additionally, participants frequently suggested that they believed foreign governments had influenced the perceptions of other voters, even though they often failed to acknowledge that their own decision-making process may have been compromised as well. However, the data in this study did not permit drawing inferences on the severity or prevalence of cyber-meddling across regions. Thus, future research should evaluate voter perceptions of cyber-meddling and its impact on decision-making processes by assessing factors such as frequency, messaging, and information sources within specific regions where participants have cast their votes.

It is important to note that this study did not assess party affiliations or categorize participants by urban or suburban areas. In many jurisdictions, where someone lives may have a stronger impact on their voting behavior than other factors. Similarly, party affiliations may often influence voters to cast their vote as expected despite concerns regarding the involvement of foreign actors in their decision-making process. Therefore, future research should also consider these additional socio-economic factors to better understand which groups of voters may be affected by cyber-meddling and why. Merely acknowledging that cyber-meddling takes place without taking action to reduce its influence on personal decision-making processes will only embolden foreign actors. Thus, additional future research should focus on how to persuade voters to make independent decisions.

Although this study confirmed the widespread use of cyber-meddling in government elections since 2016, it also uncovered discrepancies among some participant responses. Future research should examine whether participants who were aware of cyber-meddling but claimed they were not influenced by it are prevalent and whether this resistance to influence is linked to recent public discussions about foreign election interference or if these individuals have always been able to identify misinformation and remain unaffected by it since 2016. Similarly, further research should explore the relationship between educational background and its impact on the effectiveness of cyber-meddling. While better-educated participants in this study were more likely to acknowledge cyber-meddling, the study's design did not permit an assessment of mitigating factors, such as peer influence, specific news sources, or geographical locations.

Conclusions

The primary objective of this research was to explore potential linkages between voters' belief in foreign governments' involvement in cyber manipulation of elections and its subsequent influence on their political decision-making. Through the framework of social cognitive theory (Bandura, 1986, 2001), the research hypothesized that since 2016, voters have been subjected to cyber manipulation, with certain segments experiencing a significant impact on their decision-making due to this interference. Most survey respondents agreed that cyber interference has been a recurring event since 2016, regardless of their geographical voting area. Additionally, many participants expressed their belief that these disinformation campaigns have influenced voter decisions, potentially leading to governments that may not accurately represent the people's will.

Despite demonstrating a link between cyber interference and its perceived influence on voter decisions in government elections post-2016, these connections were inconsistent across the entire participant population. Factors such as geographical location of voting, age, race, and education level proved to be influential determinants in participants' responses to the study. The results of this study underscore the need for further exploration into how cyber interference shapes the beliefs and behaviors of voters in government elections across various factors, such as ideologies, party affiliations, and social networks. Given the continued prevalence of these disinformation campaigns, it is reasonable to infer that the orchestrators of these initiatives perceive them to be effective.

Merely being aware of a disinformation campaign does not necessarily diminish its impact on voters' decision-making processes. Furthermore, this study did not assess the accuracy of perceived misinformation. Some participants may have mistaken opinions or facts that do not align with their beliefs as misinformation, even though they may have been closer to the truth than the alternative. Thus, merely labeling certain information as misinformation does not validate the quality, or lack thereof, of that information. Instead, it reflects a deeply rooted social cognitive experience that continues to shape voter perceptions, even in the absence of cyber-meddling.

References

Abutabenjeh, S., & Jaradat, R. (2018). Clarification of research design, research methods, and research methodology: A guide for public administration researchers and practitioners. *Teaching Public Administration, 36,* 237-258. https://doi.org/10.1177/0144739418775787

Agrawal, N. (2020). *The digital challenges to democracy: Social media and new information paradigms* [PhD Thesis, International Institute of Information Technology Hyderabad].

Ahmad, F., & Khan Sherwani, R. A. (2015). Power comparison of various normality tests [Article]. *Pakistan Journal of Statistics & Operation Research, 11,* 331-345. https://doi.org/10.18187/pjsor.v11i3.1082

Ajzen, I. (1991). The theory of planned behavior. *Organizational Behavior and Human Decision Processes, 50*(2), 179-211. https://doi.org/10.1016/0749-5978(91)90020-T

Alashri, S., Kandala, S. S., Bajaj, V., Ravi, R., Smith, K. L., & Desouza, K. C. (2016). An analysis of sentiments on facebook during the 2016 u.S. Presidential election. 2016 IEEE/ACM International Conference on Advances in Social Networks Analysis and Mining (ASONAM),

Allcott, H., & Gentzkow, M. (2017). Social media and fake news in the 2016 election. *Journal of Economic Perspectives, 31*(2), 211-236. https://doi.org/10.1257/jep.31.2.211

Allcott, H., Gentzkow, M., & Yu, C. (2019). *Trends in the diffusion of misinformation on social media* (w25500). http://www.nber.org/papers/w25500.pdf

Altman, N., & Krzywinski, M. (2016). Points of significance: Analyzing outliers: Influential or nuisance? *Nature Methods, 13*, 281-282. https://doi.org/10.1038/nmeth.3812

Alwagait, E., Shahzad, B., & Alim, S. (2015). Impact of social media usage on students academic performance in saudi arabia. *Computers in Human Behavior, 51*, 1092-1097. https://doi.org/10.1016/j.chb.2014.09.028

Arquilla, J., & Guzdial, M. (2017). Crafting a national cyberdefense, and preparing to support computational literacy. *Communications of the ACM, 60*(4), 10-11. https://doi.org/10.1145/3048379

Bagya Lakshmi, H., Gallo, M., & Srinivasan, M. R. (2018). Comparison of regression models under multicollinearity [Article]. *Electronic Journal of Applied Statistical Analysis, 11*, 340-368. https://doi.org/10.1285/i20705948v11n1p340

Baines, P., & Jones, N. (2018). Influence and interference in foreign elections. https://doi.org/10.1080/03071847.2018.1446723

Bandura, A. (1977). Self-efficacy: Toward a unifying theory of behavioral change. *Psychological review, 84*(2), 191. https://doi.org/10.1037/0033-295x.84.2.191

Bandura, A. (1986). Social foundations of thought and action. *Englewood Cliffs, NJ, 1986* (23-28).

Bandura, A. (2001). Social cognitive theory of mass communication. *Media psychology, 3*(3), 265-299. https://doi.org/10.1207/s1532785xmep0303_03

Bandura, A. (2018). Toward a psychology of human agency: Pathways and reflections. *Perspectives on psychological science, 13*(2), 130-136. https://doi.org/10.1177/1745691617699280

Bandura, A., & Walters, R. H. (1963). Social learning and personality development.

Bandura, A., & Walters, R. H. (1977). *Social learning theory* (Vol. 1). Englewood cliffs Prentice Hall.

Banks, W. (2017). State responsibility and attribution of cyber intrusions after tallinn 2.0. *Texas Law Review, 95*(7), 1487-1514.

Baram, G., Paikowsky, D., Pavel, T., & Ben-Israel, I. (2017). *Trends in government cyber security activities in 2016* [SSRN Scholarly Paper](ID 3113106). https://papers.ssrn.com/sol3/papers.cfm?abstract_id=3113106

Benkler, Y., Farris, R., & Roberts, H. (2018). *Network propaganda* (Vol. 1). Oxford University Press. http://www.oxfordscholarship.com/view/10.1093/oso/9780190923624.001.0001/oso-9780190923624

Bernstein, J. L. (2018). Unifying sotl methodology: Internal and external validity. *Teaching & Learning Inquiry, 6*, 115-126. https://doi.org/10.20343/teachlearninqu.6.2.9

Bobak, C. A., Barr, P. J., & O'Malley, A. J. (2018). Estimation of an inter-rater intra-class correlation coefficient that overcomes common assumption violations in the assessment of health measurement scales. *BMC MEDICAL RESEARCH METHODOLOGY, 18*(1), 93-104. https://doi.org/10.1186/s12874-018-0550-6

Bolarinwa, O. A. (2015). Principles and methods of validity and reliability testing of questionnaires used in social and health science researches. *Nigerian Postgraduate Medical Journal, 22*, 195-201. https://doi.org/10.4103/1117-1936.173959

Bollmann, H.-S., & Gibeon, G. (2022). *The spread of hacked materials on twitter: A threat to democracy? A case study of the 2017 macron leaks* [Doctoral Dissertation, Hertie School].

Bradshaw, S., & Howard, P. N. (2018). The global organization of social media disinformation campaigns. *Journal of International Affairs, 71*(1.5), 23-32.

Bradshaw, S., Kollanyi, B., Desigaud, C., & Bolsover, G. (2017). *Junk news and bots during the french presidential election: What are french voters sharing over twitter?*

Braun, D., & Tausendpfund, M. (2020). Electoral behaviour in a european union under stress. *Politics and Governance*(1), 28-40. https://doi.org/10.17645/pag.v8i1.2510

Burke, M., & Hodgins, M. (2015). Is 'dear colleague' enough? Improving response rates in surveys of healthcare professionals [Report]. *Nurse Researcher, 23*(1), 8-15. https://doi.org/10.7748/nr.23.1.8.e1339

Burr, R., Warner, M., Collins, S., Heinrich, M., & Lankford, J. (2018). *Senate intel committee releases unclassified 1st installment in russia report, updated recommendations on election security.* https://www.justsecurity.org/wp-content/uploads/2019/03/5.8.18-Statement-on-SSCI-Report.pdf

Cacioppo, J. T., & Petty, R. E. (1986). The elaboration likelihood model of persuasion. In *Communication and*

persuasion (pp. 1-24). Springer.
https://doi.org/10.1007/978-1-4612-4964-1_1

Cadwalladr, C., & Graham-Harrison, E. (2018). Revealed: 50 million facebook profiles harvested for cambridge analytica in major data breach. *The Guardian.* https://www.theguardian.com/news/2018/mar/17/cambridge-analytica-facebook-influence-us-election files/232/cambridge-analytica-facebook-influence-us-election.html

Cahill, P. (2017). *Cheney says russian meddling in u.S. Election possibly an 'act of war'.* NBC News. https://www.nbcnews.com/politics/white-house/dick-cheney-russian-election-interference-could-be-seen-act-war-n739391

Caprara, G. V., Vecchione, M., Capanna, C., & Mebane, M. (2009). Perceived political self-efficacy: Theory, assessment, and applications. *European journal of social psychology, 39*(6), 1002-1020. https://doi.org/10.1002/ejsp.604

Chen, X., Sin, S. C. J., Theng, Y. L., & Lee, C. S. (2015). Deterring the spread of misinformation on social network sites: A social cognitive theory-guided intervention. *Proceedings of the Association for Information Science and Technology, 52*(1), 1-4. https://doi.org/10.1002/pra2.2015.145052010095

Choudhary, P. K., Syal, R., & Arora, T. (2020). Do issues matter in indian elections. *IPP Indian Politics & Policy, 3*(1), 31-48. https://doi.org/10.18278/inpp.3.1.4

Chyung, S. Y., Roberts, K., Swanson, I., & Hankinson, A. (2017). Evidence-based survey design: The use of a midpoint on the likert scale [Article]. *Performance Improvement, 56*(10), 15-23. https://doi.org/10.1002/pfi.21727

CoŞKuntuncel, O. o. m. e. t. (2018). Bounded-influence regression estimation for mixture experiments [Article]. *Karma Denemelerde Sınırlı Etkili Regresyon Tahmin Edicileri., 14*, 1020-1037. https://doi.org/10.17860/mersinefd.443584

Costanza, D. P., Blacksmith, N., & Coats, M. (2015). Convenience samples and teaching organizational research methods [Article]. *The Industrial-Organizational Psychologist, 53*(1), 137-140. http://my.siop.org/tipdefault

Creswell, J. W. (2014). *Research design: Qualitative, quantitative, and mixed methods approaches* (4th edition, international student edition ed.). SAGE.

Department of Justice. (2021). *Two iranian nationals charged for cyber-enabled disinformation and threat campaign designed to influence the 2020 u.S. Presidential election.* Department of Justice. https://www.justice.gov/opa/pr/two-iranian-nationals-charged-cyber-enabled-disinformation-and-threat-campaign-designed

Downing, J., & Ahmed, W. (2019). Macronleaks as a "warning shot" for European democracies: Challenges to election blackouts presented by social media and election meddling during the 2017 french presidential election. *French Politics, 17*, 257-278. https://doi.org/10.1057/s41253-019-00090-w

East, R. (2015). Bias in the evaluation of research methods. *Marketing Theory, 16*, 219-231. https://doi.org/10.1177/1470593115609797

Ebert, J. F., Huibers, L., Christensen, B., & Christensen, M. B. (2018). Paper- or web-based questionnaire invitations as a method for data collection: Cross-sectional comparative study of differences in response rate, completeness of data, and financial cost. *JOURNAL OF MEDICAL INTERNET RESEARCH, 20*(1), 1-13. https://doi.org/10.2196/jmir.8353

Ellehuus, R., & Ruy, D. (2020). Did russia influence brexit? https://www.csis.org/blogs/brexit-bits-bobs-and-blogs/did-russia-influence-brexit

Farkas, J., & Bastos, M. (2018). Ira propaganda on twitter: Stoking antagonism and tweeting local news. Proceedings of the 9th International Conference on social media and society, Copenhagen, Denmark.

Fidler, D. P. (2016). The u.S. Election hacks, cybersecurity, and international law. *AJIL Unbound, 110*, 337-342. https://doi.org/10.1017/aju.2017.5

Flick, U. (2016). Mantras and myths: The disenchantment of mixed-methods research and revisiting triangulation as a perspective. *Qualitative Inquiry, 23*(1), 46-57. https://doi.org/10.1177/1077800416655827

Flower, A., McKenna, J. W., & Upreti, G. (2015). Validity and reliability of graphclick and datathief iii for data extraction. *Behavior Modification, 40*, 396-413. https://doi.org/10.1177/0145445515616105

Fogarty, G. J., Perera, H. N., Furst, A. J., & Thomas, P. R. (2016). Evaluating measures of optimism and sport confidence. *Measurement in Physical Education and Exercise Science, 20*(2), 81-92. https://doi.org/10.1080/1091367X.2015.1111220

Fowler, F. J. (2009). *Survey research methods* (4. ed ed.). SAGE.

Frimer, J. A., Skitka, L. J., & Motyl, M. (2017). Liberals and conservatives are similarly motivated to avoid exposure to one another's opinions. *Journal of Experimental Social Psychology, 72*, 1-12. https://doi.org/10.1016/j.jesp.2017.04.003

Garrett, R. K. (2019). Social media's contribution to political misperceptions in u.S. Presidential elections. *PLOS ONE, 14*(3), e0213500. https://doi.org/10.1371/journal.pone.0213500

Gaumont, N., Panahi, M., & Chavalarias, D. (2018). Reconstruction of the socio-semantic dynamics of political activist twitter networks—method and application to the 2017 french presidential election. *PLOS ONE, 13*(9), e0201879. https://doi.org/10.1371/journal.pone.0201879

Giglietto, F., Iannelli, L., Rossi, L., & Valeriani, A. (2016). *Fakes, news and the election: A new taxonomy for the study of misleading information within the hybrid media system* [SSRN Scholarly Paper](ID 2878774). https://papers.ssrn.com/sol3/papers.cfm?abstract_id=287877 4

Green, S. B., & Salkind, N. J. (2016). *Using spss for windows and macintosh : Analyzing and understanding data.* Pearson.

Grinberg, N., Joseph, K., Friedland, L., Swire-Thompson, B., & Lazer, D. (2019). Fake news on twitter during the 2016 u.S. Presidential election. *Science, 363*(6425), 374-378. https://doi.org/10.1126/science.aau2706

Guess, A., Nagler, J., & Tucker, J. (2019). Less than you think: Prevalence and predictors of fake news dissemination on facebook. *Science Advances, 5*(1), eaau4586. https://doi.org/10.1126/sciadv.aau4586

Haegele, J. A., & Hodge, S. R. (2015). Quantitative methodology: A guide for emerging physical education and adapted physical education researchers [Article]. *Physical Educator, 72*(5), 59-75. https://doi.org/10.18666/tpe-2015-v72-i5-6133

Hales, A. H. (2016). Does the conclusion follow from the evidence? Recommendations for improving research. *Journal of Experimental Social Psychology, 66*, 39-46. https://doi.org/10.1016/j.jesp.2015.09.011

Harkiolakis, N. (2017). *Quantitative research methods: From theory to publication.* CreateSpace Independent Publishing Platform.

Harrison, S. (2018). Young voters. *Parliamentary Affairs, 71*(suppl_1), 255-266. https://doi.org/10.1093/pa/gsx068

Hasen, R. L. (2017). *The 2016 u.S. Voting wars: From bad to worse* [SSRN Scholarly Paper](ID 3001257). https://papers.ssrn.com/abstract=3001257 files/245/papers.html

Hashim, N. H., Mat Desa, W. N. S., & Ismail, D. (2018). Pearson product moment correlation (ppmc) and principal component analysis (pca) for objective comparison and source determination of unbranded black ballpoint pen inks au - mohamad asri, muhammad naeim. *Australian Journal of Forensic Sciences, 50*, 323-340. https://doi.org/10.1080/00450618.2016.1236292

Heale, R., & Twycross, A. (2015). Validity and reliability in quantitative studies. *Evidence-based nursing, 18*(3), 66-67. https://doi.org/10.1136/eb-2015-102129

Hicks, T. (2018). Defending and recovering american election systems. *Brown Journal of World Affairs, 24*(2), 97-108.

Hjelmgaard, K. (2016). *Russian prime minister says there's a new cold war.* https://www.usatoday.com/story/news/world/2016/02/13/hje lmgaard/80334952/files/364/80334952.html

House, J. (2018). Authentic vs elicited data and qualitative vs quantitative research methods in pragmatics: Overcoming two non-fruitful dichotomies. *System, 75*, 4-12. https://doi.org/10.1016/j.system.2018.03.014

Howard, P. N., Ganesh, B., Liotsiou, D., Kelly, J., & François, C. (2019). The ira, social media and political polarization in the united states, 2012-2018. https://doi.org/10.1515/sirius-2019-1017

Howard, P. N., Woolley, S., & Calo, R. (2018). Algorithms, bots, and political communication in the us 2016 election: The challenge of automated political communication for election law and administration. *Journal of Information Technology & Politics, 15*(2), 81-93. https://doi.org/10.1080/19331681.2018.1448735

Huang, C.-C. L., Yow-Jen, J., & Hsun-Jung, C. (2016). A new multicollinearity diagnostic for generalized linear models

[Article]. *Journal of Applied Statistics, 43*, 2029-2043. https://doi.org/10.1080/02664763.2015.1126239

Huang, Z. (2018). Application of statistical inference in education and teaching. *Educational Sciences: Theory & Practice, 18*(6). https://doi.org/10.12738/estp.2018.6.179

Huddy, L., Mason, L., & Aarøe, L. (2015). Expressive partisanship: Campaign involvement, political emotion, and partisan identity. *American Political Science Review, 109*(1), 1-17. https://doi.org/10.1017/s0003055414000604

Hughes, J. L., Camden, A. A., & Yangchen, T. (2016). Rethinking and updating demographic questions: Guidance to improve descriptions of research samples. *Psi Chi Journal of Psychological Research, 21*, 138-151. https://doi.org/10.24839/b21.3.138

Hutcheson, G., & Williams, J. (2016). Handling missing data: Analysis of a challenging data set using multiple imputation au - pampaka, maria. *International Journal of Research & Method in Education, 39*, 19-37. https://doi.org/10.1080/1743727X.2014.979146

Intelligence and Security Committee of Parliament. (2020). *Russia* (HC 632). https://assets.documentcloud.org/documents/6999013/20200721-HC632-CCS001-CCS1019402408-001-ISC.pdf

Jager, J., Putnick, D. L., & Bornstein, M. H. (2017). Ii. More than just convenient: The scientific merits of homogeneous convenience samples [Article]. *Monographs of the Society for Research in Child Development, 82*(2), 13-30. https://doi.org/10.1111/mono.12296

Jalli, N., Jalli, N., & Idris, I. (2019). Fake news and elections in two southeast asian nations: A comparative study of malaysia general election 2018 and indonesia presidential election 2019. Proceedings of the International Conference of Democratisation in Southeast Asia (ICDeSA 2019),

Jarvis, R. (2018). Midterm election meddling. *World News with Diane Sawyer*, 1.

Johnson, N. R., Dzara, K., Pelletier, A., & Goldfarb, I. T. (2022). Medical students' intention to change after receiving formative feedback: Employing social cognitive theories of behavior. *Medical Science Educator*, 1-8. https://doi.org/10.1007/s40670-022-01668-w

Kahneman, D., & Tversky, A. (1979). On the interpretation of intuitive probability: A reply to jonathan cohen. *Cognition, 4*(7), 409-411. https://doi.org/10.1016/0010-0277(79)90024-6

Kalsnes, B. (2018). Fake news. In *Oxford research encyclopedia of communication*. Oxford University Press. https://oxfordre.com/communication/view/10.1093/acrefore/9780190228613.001.0001/acrefore-9780190228613-e-809

Kaltwasser, C. R., & Van Hauwaert, S. M. (2020). The populist citizen: Empirical evidence from europe and latin america. *European Political Science Review, 12*(1), 1-18. https://doi.org/10.1017/S1755773919000262

Kanev, D. (2017). *Why trump won the elections – in view of the prospect theory* [SSRN Scholarly Paper](ID 3007802). https://papers.ssrn.com/abstract=3007802

files/248/papers.html

Kazdin, A. E. (2018). Single-case experimental designs. Evaluating interventions in research and clinical practice. *Behaviour Research and Therapy.* https://doi.org/10.1016/j.brat.2018.11.015

Keusch, F. (2015). Why do people participate in web surveys? Applying survey participation theory to internet survey data collection. *Management review quarterly, 65,* 183-216. https://doi.org/10.1007/s11301-014-0111-y

Kim, R. S., Aloe, A. M., & Becker, B. J. (2017). Extracting the variance inflation factor and other multicollinearity diagnostics from typical regression results au - thompson, christopher glen. *Basic and Applied Social Psychology, 39,* 81-90. https://doi.org/10.1080/01973533.2016.1277529

Kim, Y., Dennis, J. M., & Kerr, C. (2017). Assessing representativeness of kernels using descriptive statistics. 2017 IEEE International Conference on Cluster Computing (CLUSTER),

Klofstad, C. A., Sokhey, A. E., & McClurg, S. D. (2013). Disagreeing about disagreement: How conflict in social networks affects political behavior. *American Journal of Political Science, 57*(1), 120-134. https://doi.org/10.1111/j.1540-5907.2012.00620.x

Kumar, R. (2011). *Research methodology : A step-by-step guide for beginners.* SAGE.

Kumar, S., & Shah, N. (2018). False information on web and social media: A survey. *arXiv:1804.08559 [cs].* http://arxiv.org/abs/1804.08559

Lent, R. W., Singley, D., Sheu, H.-B., Schmidt, J. A., & Schmidt, L. C. (2007). Relation of social-cognitive factors to academic satisfaction in engineering students. *Journal of Career Assessment, 15*(1), 87-97. https://doi.org/10.1177/1069072706294518

Leung, S.-O. (2011). A comparison of psychometric properties and normality in 4-, 5-, 6-, and 11-point likert scales. *Journal of Social Service Research, 37*, 412-421. https://doi.org/10.1080/01488376.2011.580697

Lewis, P., & Hilder, P. (2018). Leaked: Cambridge analytica's blueprint for trump victory. *The Guardian.* https://www.theguardian.com/uk-news/2018/mar/23/leaked-cambridge-analyticas-blueprint-for-trump-victory files/233/leaked-cambridge-analyticas-blueprint-for-trump-victory.html

Loomis, D. K., & Paterson, S. (2018). A comparison of data collection methods: Mail versus online surveys. *Journal of Leisure Research, 49*, 133-149. https://doi.org/10.1080/00222216.2018.1494418

López, M. T. C., Ponce-Espinosa, G., Rios-Zaruma, J., & Espinoza-Torres, D. (2018). Reliability analysis of a measurement instrument of organizational capacities in the commercial sector. 2018 13th Iberian Conference on Information Systems and Technologies (CISTI),

Lühnen, J., Mühlhauser, I., & Steckelberg, A. (2018). The quality of informed consent forms--a systematic review and critical analysis [Article]. *Deutsches Aerzteblatt International, 115*, 377-383. https://doi.org/10.3238/arztebl.2018.0377

Lysenko, V., & Brooks, C. (2018). Russian information troops, disinformation, and democracy. *First Monday.* https://doi.org/10.5210/fm.v22i5.8176

Marquart, F., Goldberg, A. C., & de Vreese, C. H. (2020). 'This time i'm (not) voting': A comprehensive overview of campaign factors influencing turnout at european parliament elections. *European Union Politics, 21*(4), 680-705. https://doi.org/10.1177/1465116520943670

Mayr, S., Buchner, A., Erdfelder, E., & Faul, F. (2007). A short tutorial of gpower. *Tutorials in Qantitatuve Methods for Psychology, 3*(2), 51-59.

McDevitt, M., & Kiousis, S. (2006). Experiments in political socialization: Kids voting USA as a model for civic education reform. *Center for Information and Research on Civic Learning and Engagement (CIRCLE), University of Maryland.*

McHugh, M. L. (2013). The chi-square test of independence. *Biochemia Medica*, 143-149. https://doi.org/10.11613/bm.2013.018

Mercier, H., Rolison, J., Stragà, M., Ferrante, D., Walsh, C. R., & Girotto, V. (2017). Questioning the preparatory function of counterfactual thinking [Article]. *Memory & Cognition, 45*, 261-269. https://doi.org/10.3758/s13421-016-0660-5

Miller, D. C., & Salkind, N. J. (2002). *Handbook of research design and social measurement.* Sage.

Morell, M., & Kelly, S. (2016). Fmr. Cia acting dir. Michael morell:'This is the political equivalent of 9/11.'. *The Cipher Brief.*

Morris, S. G. (2020). Empathy and the liberal-conservative political divide in the us. *Journal of Social and Political Psychology, 8*(1), 8-24. https://doi.org/10.5964/jspp.v8i1.1102

Moser, A., & Korstjens, I. (2018). Series: Practical guidance to qualitative research. Part 3: Sampling, data collection and analysis. *The European Journal Of General Practice, 24*(1), 9-18. https://doi.org/10.1080/13814788.2017.1375091

Mueller, R. S. (2019a). *The mueller report*. MUSAICUM Books.

Mueller, R. S. (2019b). *Report on the investigation into russian interference in the 2016 presidential election* (Vol. 1). US Department of Justice Washington, DC.

Norris, P. (2016). *Why american elections are flawed (and how to fix them)*. Cornell University Press. https://doi.org/10.7591/cornell/9781501713408.001.0001

Office of the Director of National Intelligence. (2017). *Assessing russian activities and intentions in recent us elections*. National Intelligence Council. https://www.intelligence.senate.gov/sites/default/files/documents/ICA_2017_01.pdf

Ohlin, J. D. (2020). *Election interference: International law and the future of democracy*. Cambridge University Press.

Okolikj, M., & Quinlan, S. (2016). Context matters: Economic voting in the 2009 and 2014 european parliament elections. *Politics and Governance, 4*(1), 145-166. https://doi.org/10.17645/pag.v4i1.458

Pal, N., & Lin, J.-J. (2017). A revisit to test the equality of variances of several populations au - chang, ching-hui.

Communications in Statistics - Simulation and Computation, 46, 6360-6384. https://doi.org/10.1080/03610918.2016.1202277

Park, J., & Park, M. (2016). Qualitative versus quantitative research methods: Discovery or justification? [Article]. *Journal of Marketing Thought, 3*(1), 1-7. https://doi.org/10.15577/jmt.2016.03.01.1

Peters, M. A. (2017). The information wars, fake news and the end of globalisation. *Educational Philosophy and Theory*, 1-4. https://doi.org/10.1080/00131857.2017.1417200

Pingree, R. J., Brossard, D., & McLeod, D. M. (2014). Effects of journalistic adjudication on factual beliefs, news evaluations, information seeking, and epistemic political efficacy. *Mass Communication and Society, 17*(5), 615-638. https://doi.org/0.1080/15205436.2013.821491

Plonsky, L., & Oswald, F. L. (2017). Multiple regression as a flexible alternative to anova in l2 research. *Studies in Second Language Acquisition, 39*, 579-592. https://doi.org/10.1017/S0272263116000231

Podsakoff, P. M., & Podsakoff, N. P. (2018). Experimental designs in management and leadership research: Strengths, limitations, and recommendations for improving publishability. *The Leadership Quarterly.* https://doi.org/10.1016/j.leaqua.2018.11.002

Powell, G. B., & Powell Jr, G. B. (2000). *Elections as instruments of democracy: Majoritarian and proportional visions.* Yale University Press.

Rennó, L. R. (2020). The bolsonaro voter: Issue positions and vote choice in the 2018 brazilian presidential elections.

Latin American Politics and Society, 62(4), 1-23.
https://doi.org/10.1017/lap.2020.13

Rensink, R. A. (2017). The nature of correlation perception in scatterplots. *Psychonomic Bulletin & Review, 24*, 776-797. https://doi.org/10.3758/s13423-016-1174-7

Robinson, M., Jones, K., & Janicke, H. (2015). Cyber warfare: Issues and challenges. *Computers & Security, 49*, 70-94. https://doi.org/10.1016/j.cose.2014.11.007

Rosenzweig, P. (2020). The capitol insurrection and pineapples on pizza. *Journal of National Security Law & Policy, 11*, 1-3.

Ruck, D. J., Rice, N. M., Borycz, J., & Bentley, R. A. (2019). Internet research agency twitter activity predicted 2016 u.S. Election polls. *First Monday*. https://doi.org/10.5210/fm.v24i7.10107

Rundle, J. (2022). Companies face stricter cyber rules in 2022. *Wall Street Journal*. https://www.wsj.com/articles/companies-face-stricter-cyber-rules-in-2022-11641205804 files/406/companies-face-stricter-cyber-rules-in-2022-11641205804.html

Rutberg, S., & Bouikidis, C. D. (2018). Exploring the evidence. Focusing on the fundamentals: A simplistic differentiation between qualitative and quantitative research. *Nephrology Nursing Journal, 45*, 209-213.

Said, M. G., Rahman, A. U., & Yousufi, M. (2021). The impact of religion on voting behavior. *Humanities & Social Sciences Reviews, 9*(2), 14-24. https://doi.org/10.18510/hssr.2021.922

Sander, B. (2019). Democracy under the influence: Paradigms of state responsibility for cyber influence operations on elections. *Chinese Journal of International Law, 18*(1), 1-56. https://doi.org/10.1093/chinesejil/jmz003

Savela, T. (2018). The advantages and disadvantages of quantitative methods in schoolscape research. *Linguistics and Education, 44*, 31-44. https://doi.org/10.1016/j.linged.2017.09.004

Schafer Astroth, K. (2018). Exploring the evidence. Focusing on the fundamentals: Reading quantitative research with a critical eye [Article]. *Nephrology Nursing Journal, 45*, 283-286.

Schia, N. N., & Gjesvik, L. (2020). Hacking democracy: Managing influence campaigns and disinformation in the digital age. *Journal of Cyber Policy, 5*(3), 413-428. https://doi.org/10.1080/23738871.2020.1820060

Schmidt, A. F., & Finan, C. (2018). Linear regression and the normality assumption. *Journal of clinical epidemiology, 98*, 146-151. https://doi.org/10.1016/j.jclinepi.2017.12.006

Schmitt, M. N. (2021). Foreign cyber interference in elections. *International Law Studies, 97*.

Schmitt, M. N., & Watts, S. (2021). Collective cyber countermeasures? *Harvard National Security Journal, 12*(2), 373-411.

Schoonenboom, J. (2018). Designing mixed methods research by mixing and merging methodologies: A 13-step model. *American Behavioral Scientist, 62*, 998-1015. https://doi.org/10.1177/0002764218772674

Schrauf, R. W. (2017). Mixed methods designs for making cross-cultural comparisons. *Journal of Mixed Methods Research, 12*, 477-494.
https://doi.org/10.1177/1558689817743109

Schunk, D. H. (1987). Self-efficacy and cognitive achievement *Annual Meeting of the*
American Psychological Association, New York.
https://files.eric.ed.gov/fulltext/ED287880.pdf

Schunk, D. H., & DiBenedetto, M. K. (2016). Self-efficacy theory in education. In *Handbook of motivation at school* (pp. 34-54). Routledge.

Schunk, D. H., & Usher, E. L. (2019). Social cognitive theory and motivation. In *The oxford handbook of human motivation* (pp. 9-26).
https://doi.org/10.1093/oxfordhb/9780190666453.013.2

Sharma, A. (2017). Fake news: A new trending phenomenon and challenges. *3*(6), 7.

Spector, P. E., & Meier, L. L. (2014). Methodologies for the study of organizational behavior processes: How to find your keys in the dark. *Journal of Organizational Behavior, 35*, 1109-1119. https://doi.org/10.1002/job.1966

Stedmon, N. (2020). The impact of cyber security threats on the 2020 us elections. *Cyber Security and Human Factors*.

Streitwieser, B., Bryant, F. B., Drane, D., & Light, G. (2019). Assessing student conceptions of international experience: Developing a validated survey instrument. *International Journal of Intercultural Relations, 68*, 26-43.
https://doi.org/10.1016/j.ijintrel.2018.10.004

Sugiura, L., Wiles, R., & Pope, C. (2016). Ethical challenges in online research: Public/private perceptions. *Research Ethics, 13*, 184-199. https://doi.org/10.1177/1747016116650720

Sullo, H. (2020). New friend request: Russia, cyber-warfare, and the threat to u.S. Elections. *FAU Undergraduate Law Journal*, 134-134. https://journals.flvc.org/FAU_UndergraduateLawJournal/article/view/121978
files/297/121978.html

Taguchi, N. (2018). Description and explanation of pragmatic development: Quantitative, qualitative, and mixed methods research. *System, 75*, 23-32. https://doi.org/10.1016/j.system.2018.03.010

Tenove, C., Buffie, J., McKay, S., & Moscrop, D. (2018). Digital threats to democratic elections: How foreign actors use digital techniques to undermine democracy. *SSRN Electronic Journal*. https://doi.org/10.2139/ssrn.3235819

Thomas, J. R., Silverman, S. J., & Nelson, J. K. (2015). *Research methods in physical activity 7th edition*. Human Kinetics.

Tomz, M., & Weeks, J. L. (2020). Public opinion and foreign electoral intervention. *American Political Science Review, 114*(3), 856-873. https://doi.org/10.1017/s0003055420000064

Torre, D. M., & Picho, K. (2016). Threats to internal and external validity in health professions education research. *Academic Medicine, 91*, e21. https://doi.org/10.1097/acm.0000000000001446

United States Census Bureau. (2022). *Population estimates, july 1, 2022 (v2022).* https://www.census.gov/quickfacts/fact/table/US/PST04522 2

Valentino, N. A., Gregorowicz, K., & Groenendyk, E. W. (2009). Efficacy, emotions and the habit of participation. *Political behavior, 31*, 307-330. https://doi.org/10.1007/s11109-008-9076-7

Van Elsas, E. J., Goldberg, A. C., & de Vreese, C. H. (2019). Eu issue voting and the 2014 european parliament elections: A dynamic perspective. *Journal of Elections, Public Opinion and Parties, 29*(3), 341-360. https://doi.org/10.1080/17457289.2018.1531009

Velasquez, A., & Quenette, A. M. (2018). Facilitating social media and offline political engagement during electoral cycles: Using social cognitive theory to explain political action among hispanics and latinos. *Mass Communication and Society, 21*(6), 763-784. https://doi.org/10.1080/15205436.2018.1484489

Vigdor, N. (2019). Federal election commissioner posts foreign interference memo on twitter. *The New York Times.* https://www.nytimes.com/2019/09/29/us/fec-chairwoman-twitter-memo.html

Vilmer, J.-B. J., & Conley, H. A. (2018). Successfully countering russian electoral interference. http://csis-website-prod.s3.amazonaws.com/s3fs-public/publication/180621_Vilmer_Countering_russiam_ele ctoral_influence.pdf

Wark, R., & Webber, J. (2015). A qualitative descriptive analysis of collaboration technology in the navy [Article]. *Interdisciplinary Journal of Information, Knowledge & Management, 10*, 173-192. https://doi.org/10.28945/2313

Waterson, J. (2018). Uk fines facebook £500,000 for failing to protect user data. *The Guardian.* https://www.theguardian.com/technology/2018/oct/25/faceb ook-fined-uk-privacy-access-user-data-cambridge-analytica

Whyte, C. (2020). Cyber conflict or democracy "hacked"? How cyber operations enhance information warfare. *Journal of Cybersecurity, 6*(tyaa013). https://doi.org/10.1093/cybsec/tyaa013

Wong, J. C. (2019). Document reveals how facebook downplayed early cambridge analytica concerns. *The Guardian.* https://www.theguardian.com/technology/2019/aug/23/cam bridge-analytica-facebook-response-internal-document files/238/cambridge-analytica-facebook-response-internal-document.html

Wu, J., Estornell, A., Kong, L., & Vorobeychik, Y. (2022). Manipulating elections by changing voter perceptions. Proceedings of the Thirty-First International Joint Conference on Artificial Intelligence, Vienna, Austria.

Wu, L., Morstatter, F., Carley, K. M., & Liu, H. (2019). Misinformation in social media: Definition, manipulation, and detection. *ACM SIGKDD explorations newsletter, 21*(2), 80-90. https://doi.org/10.1145/3373464.3373475

Yang, Y., Ding, Y., & Zhao, Z. (2017). Fault distribution analysis of airborne equipment based on probability plot.

2017 3rd IEEE International Conference on Control Science and Systems Engineering (ICCSSE),

Yilmaz, K. (2013). Comparison of quantitative and qualitative research traditions: Epistemological, theoretical, and methodological differences. *European Journal of Education, 48*, 311-325. https://doi.org/10.1111/ejed.12014

Yoon, H.-J., & Tourassi, G. (2014). Analysis of online social networks to understand information sharing behaviors through social cognitive theory. Proceedings of the 2014 Biomedical Sciences and Engineering Conference, Oak Ridge, Tennessee, USA.

Zimmerman, B. J., & Schunk, D. H. (2004). Self-regulating intellectual processes and outcomes: A social cognitive perspective. In *Motivation, emotion, and cognition* (pp. 337-364). Routledge. https://doi.org/10.4324/9781410610515-22

Zyphur, M., & Pierides, D. (2017). Is quantitative research ethical? Tools for ethically practicing, evaluating, and using quantitative research [Article]. *Journal of Business Ethics, 143*, 1-16. https://doi.org/10.1007/s10551-017-3549-8

Appendix A:
Questionnaire

Informed Consent and Study Introduction

Please complete the questionnaire if you have voted in any governmental election since 2016. No personally identifiable information is collected, and you are free to stop or leave at any time you want.

	Question	Dropdown options
D1	What is your gender?	a. User input text box
D2	What is your age?	a. 18-30 b. 31-40 c. 41-50 d. 51-60 e. Over 60
D3	What is your race?	a. User input text box
D4	What is your highest level of education?	a. Middle School b. High School (No Diploma) c. High School Graduate (or equivalent) d. Some College Credit (No Degree) e. Trade/Technical/Vocational Training f. Associate Degree g. Bachelor's Degree h. Master's Degree i. Professional Degree j. Doctorate Degree k. None of the above
D5	In which country did you most recently cast your vote in a governmental election	a. Asia b. Australia c. Eastern Europe d. Western Europe e. Africa f. North America g. South America h. Other

D6	During how many governmental elections in your region did you vote since 2016?	a. Once b. Multiple Times
D7	Which social media accounts do you frequently use (click all that apply) to learn about political candidates and parties during election periods since 2016?	a. Facebook (Meta) b. Twitter c. Instagram d. TikTok e. Reddit f. YouTube g. LinkedIn h. Discord i. Other
D8	Which traditional media do you frequently use/read (click all that apply) to learn about political candidates and parties during election periods since 2016?	a. Cable b. Radio c. Newspaper d. Other e. None

Appendix A. Demographics.

Justification: Asking participants demographic questions informs multiple research objectives: a) it ensures that participants are qualified and come from the desired population, and b) it assists researchers in categorizing responses into meaningful groups (Fowler, 2009).

Subject Matter Questions on Voter Perception of Cyber-Meddling by Foreign Governments

As someone who has perceived cyber-election meddling and voted in a recent governmental election, please select your level of agreement with the following statements:

Questions to identify exposure to cyber-meddling by foreign governments as perceived by voters who cast a ballot during recent government elections (RQ1).

Q1. For information about political candidates and their programs in government elections since 2016 I rely on traditional media such as cable, radio, or newspapers.

Strongly Disagree	Disagree	Neither Agree nor Disagree	Agree	Strongly Agree

Justification: In relation to RQ1, this question offers insights into whether the participant has been exposed to political ads on traditional media, some of which may be paid for by foreign government operations in an attempt to influence voters (Benkler et al., 2018; Lysenko & Brooks, 2018; Sharma, 2017).

Q2. For information about political candidates and their programs in government elections since 2016 I rely on non-traditional media such as social network sites or blog posts.

Strongly Disagree	Disagree	Neither Agree nor Disagree	Agree	Strongly Agree

Justification: In relation to RQ1, this question offers insights into whether the participant has been exposed to political ads on non-traditional media, some of which may be paid for by foreign government operations in an attempt to influence voters (Benkler et al., 2018; Lysenko & Brooks, 2018; Sharma, 2017).

Q3. I believe what is presented in traditional media like cable, radio, or newspapers about political candidates and their programs in government elections since 2016 can be misleading.

Strongly Disagree	Disagree	Neither Agree nor Disagree	Agree	Strongly Agree

Justification: In relation to RQ1, this question offers insights into whether participants believe that established news organizations report mostly accurately. Some researchers suggest that distrust in established organizations can amplify tendencies to look for alternative news sources, regardless of whether these sources report accurately or not (Benkler et al., 2018; Bradshaw et al., 2017; Kalsnes, 2018; Kumar & Shah, 2018; Pingree et al., 2014; Sullo, 2020).

Q4. I believe what is presented in non-traditional media like social media or blog posts about political candidates and their programs in government elections since 2016 can be misleading.

Strongly Disagree	Disagree	Neither Agree nor Disagree	Agree	Strongly Agree

Justification: In relation to RQ1, this question offers insights into whether participants believe that social media or blog posts are a source for accurate news. Some researchers suggest that distrust in social media can amplify tendencies to look for established news sources, regardless of whether these sources report accurately or not (Benkler et al., 2018; Bradshaw et al., 2017; Kalsnes, 2018; Kumar & Shah, 2018; Pingree et al., 2014; Sullo, 2020).

Q5. I believe there was cyber election meddling by foreign governments since 2016 through traditional media like cable, radio, or newspapers.

Strongly Disagree	Disagree	Neither Agree nor Disagree	Agree	Strongly Agree

Justification: In relation to RQ1, this question offers insights into whether participants believe cyber-meddling on traditional media impacted the election process. As the SCT posits, learning includes factors such as retention, reproduction, and motivation, suggesting that in the context of voter decision-making process, cyber-meddling may impact learning outcomes and thus impact beliefs (Chen et al., 2015; Schunk & Usher, 2019; Sharma, 2017; Velasquez & Quenette, 2018; Zimmerman & Schunk, 2004).

Q6. I believe there was cyber election meddling by foreign governments since 2016 through non-traditional media like social media or blog posts.

Strongly Disagree	Disagree	Neither Agree nor Disagree	Agree	Strongly Agree

Justification: In relation to RQ1, this question offers insights into whether participants believe cyber-meddling on non-traditional media impacted the election process. As the SCT posits, learning includes factors such as retention, reproduction, and motivation, suggesting that in the context of voter decision-making process, cyber-meddling may impact learning outcomes and thus impact beliefs (Chen et al., 2015; Grinberg et al., 2019; Schunk & Usher, 2019; Sharma, 2017; Velasquez & Quenette, 2018; Wu et al., 2022; Zimmerman & Schunk, 2004).

Q7. I believe cyber election meddling by foreign governments since 2016 affected the voting procedures and processes.

Strongly Disagree	Disagree	Neither Agree nor Disagree	Agree	Strongly Agree

Justification: In relation to RQ1, this question offers insights into whether participants believe cyber-meddling impacted the election process by changing procedures and processes. As the SCT posits, learning includes factors such as retention, reproduction, and motivation, suggesting that in the context of voter decision-making process, cyber-meddling may impact learning outcomes and thus impact beliefs (Chen et al., 2015; Schunk & Usher, 2019; Sharma, 2017; Velasquez & Quenette, 2018; Wu et al., 2022; Zimmerman & Schunk, 2004).

Q8. I believe cyber election meddling by foreign governments might have influenced my perception about political candidates and their programs in government elections since 2016.

Strongly Disagree	Disagree	Neither Agree nor Disagree	Agree	Strongly Agree

Justification: In relation to RQ1, this question offers insights into whether participants believe cyber-meddling impacted their perception about political candidates and their programs. As the SCT posits, learning includes factors such as retention, reproduction, and motivation, suggesting that in the context of voter decision-making process (Ellehuus & Ruy, 2020; Grinberg et al., 2019; Wu et al., 2022), cyber-meddling may impact learning outcomes and thus impact beliefs (Chen et al., 2015; Schunk & Usher, 2019; Sharma, 2017; Velasquez & Quenette, 2018; Zimmerman & Schunk, 2004).

Q9. I believe cyber election meddling by foreign governments might have influenced my decision-making process in government elections since 2016.

Strongly Disagree	Disagree	Neither Agree nor Disagree	Agree	Strongly Agree

Justification: In relation to RQ1, this question offers insights into whether participants believe cyber-meddling impacted their decision-making process in government elections since 2016. As the SCT posits, learning includes factors such as retention, reproduction, and motivation, suggesting that in the context of voter decision-making process (Ellehuus & Ruy, 2020; Grinberg et al., 2019; Wu et al., 2022), cyber-meddling may impact learning outcomes and thus impact beliefs (Chen et al., 2015; Ellehuus & Ruy, 2020; Schunk & Usher, 2019; Sharma, 2017; Velasquez & Quenette, 2018; Zimmerman & Schunk, 2004).

Q10. I believe cyber election meddling by foreign governments has resulted in unfair processes in government elections since 2016.

Strongly Disagree	Disagree	Neither Agree nor Disagree	Agree	Strongly Agree

Justification: In relation to RQ1, this question offers insights into whether participants believe cyber-meddling impacted the election process by making it an unfair decision-making process. Several researchers have shown that motivation is an essential aspect of learning in the context of the SCT (Bandura, 2001; Chen et al., 2015; Schunk & Usher, 2019; Sharma, 2017; Yoon & Tourassi, 2014; Zimmerman & Schunk, 2004). Therefore, believing in unfair processes may predispose some participants to be more likely susceptible to cyber-meddling efforts (Ellehuus & Ruy, 2020; Grinberg et al., 2019; Kanev, 2017; Sullo, 2020; Wu et al., 2022).

Q11. I believe cyber election meddling by foreign governments has resulted in governments that do not represent the people.

Strongly Disagree	Disagree	Neither Agree nor Disagree	Agree	Strongly Agree

Justification: In relation to RQ1, this question offers insights into whether participants believe cyber-meddling resulted in governments that do not represent the people. Several researchers have shown that motivation and retention are essential aspects of learning in the context of the SCT (Bandura, 2001; Chen et al., 2015; Schunk & Usher, 2019; Sharma, 2017; Yoon & Tourassi, 2014; Zimmerman & Schunk, 2004). Therefore, believing that duly elected governments do not represent the people may predispose some participants to be more likely susceptible to cyber-meddling efforts (Ellehuus & Ruy, 2020; Grinberg et al., 2019; Kanev, 2017; Sullo, 2020; Wu et al., 2022).decision-making process

Appendix B:
Participant Invitation

Date: [Insert Date]

Re: Invitation to Participate in a Research Study

Dear [Insert Recipient]:

My name is Faton Aliu, and I am a doctoral student at École des Ponts, pursuing an executive Doctor of Business Administration degree (eDBA). I am conducting a research study titled "The Relationship Between Cyber Election Meddling and the Perception of Election Validity and Future Election Legitimacy." I am writing to you to request your participation in my study. Participation involves completing an anonymous brief online survey.

My study explores the relationships between voters' perception of cyber election meddling by foreign governments and their belief in its impact on their decision-making process in government elections. I want to help social media companies and governments better understand cyber-meddling's impact on voter beliefs and how to better safeguard the election processes against foreign influence. If you have voted in a governmental election in a region/country/state where you were registered to vote since 2016, I would greatly appreciate your participation in my study.

Please disregard this message if you do not wish to participate in this research. Otherwise, please complete the online survey by visiting the following [Insert Link].

I appreciate you considering participation in this study. Please feel free to reach out anytime with any questions you may have. Stay safe.

Sincerely,
Faton Aliu
eDBA Student, École des Ponts, Paris

Appendix C:
P-P Plots

	Q1	Q2	Q3	Q4	Q5
Series or Sequence Length	124	124	124	124	124
Number of Missing Values User-Missing	0	0	0	0	0
in the Plot System-Missing	0	0	0	0	0

Appendix C1. Case Processing Summary 1/3.

	Q6	Q7	Q8	Q9	Q10
Series or Sequence Length	124	124	124	124	124
Number of Missing Values User-Missing	0	0	0	0	0
in the Plot System-Missing	0	0	0	0	0

Appendix C2. Case Processing Summary 2/3.

		Q11
Series or Sequence Length		124
Number of Missing Values in the Plot	User-Missing	0
	System-Missing	0

Appendix C3. Case processing Summary 3/3.

	Q1	Q2	Q3	Q4	Q5	Q6
Normal Distribution Location	2.42	2.84	2.41	1.98	2.59	1.98
Scale	1.230	1.278	.980	.954	.963	.906

Appendix C4. Estimated Distribution Parameters 1/2

	Q7	Q8	Q9	Q10	Q11
Normal Distribution Location	2.04	3.10	3.31	2.35	2.58
Scale	.905	1.093	1.047	.912	1.037

Appendix C5. Estimated Distribution Parameters 2/2.

The cases are unweighted.

Q1

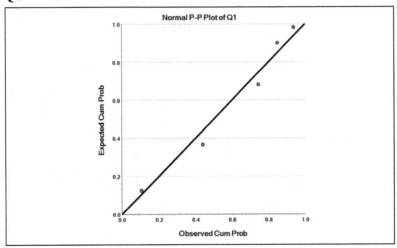

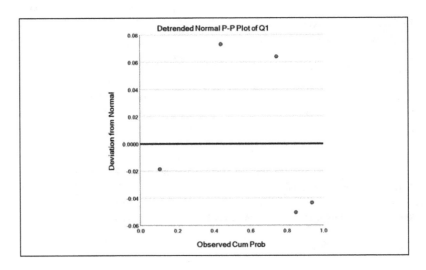

Q2

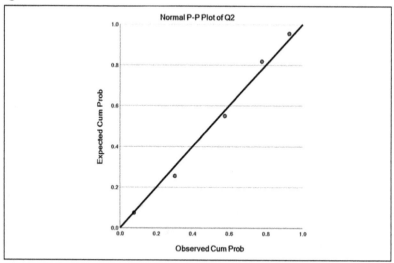

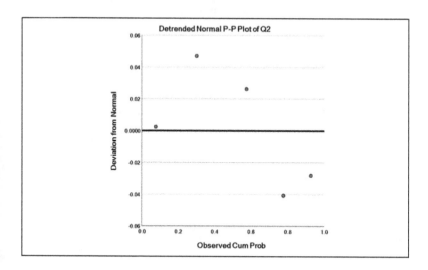

Q3

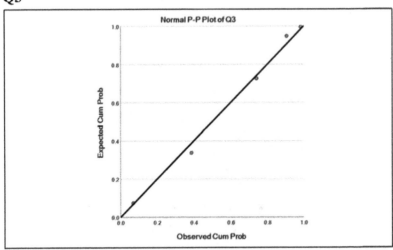

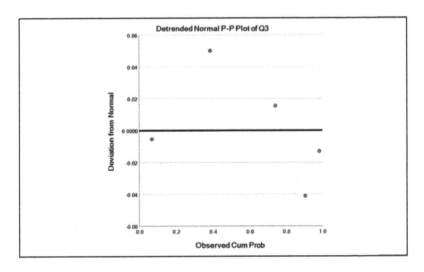

Q4

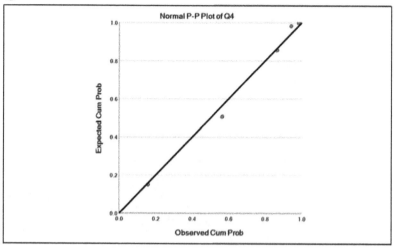

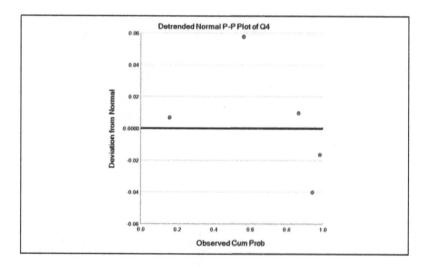

Q5

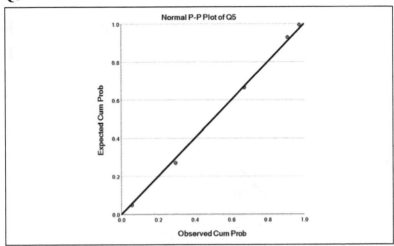

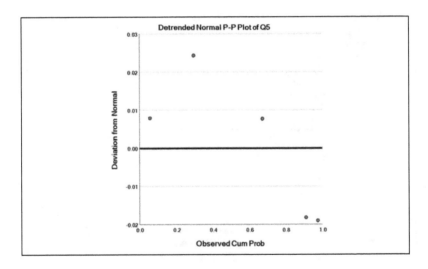

Q6

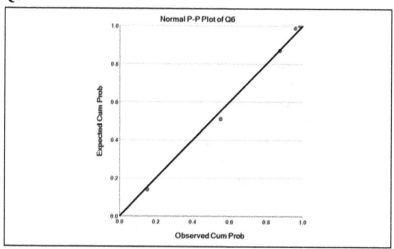

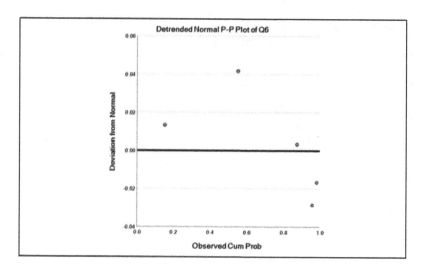

Q7

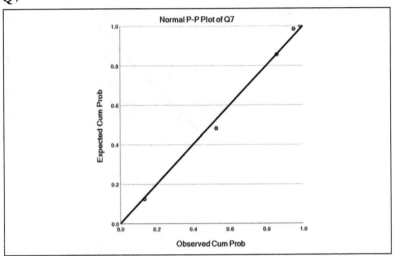

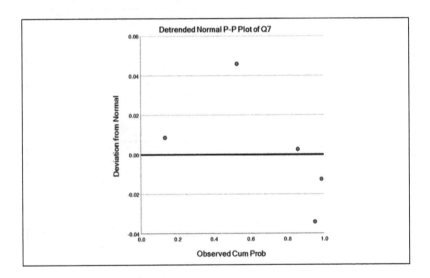

Q8

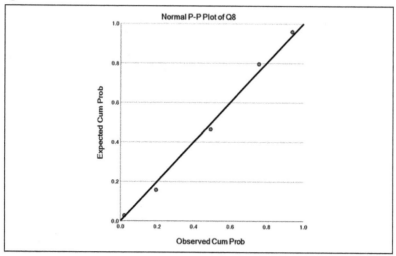

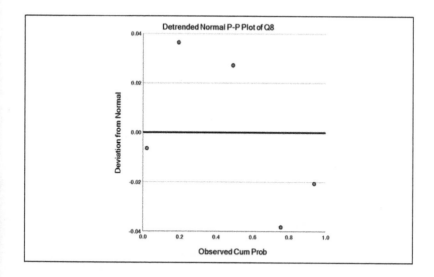

Q9

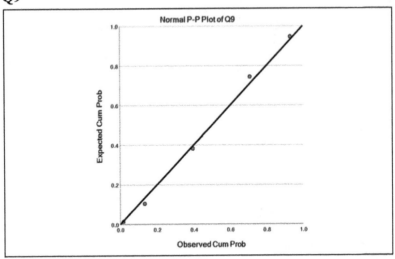

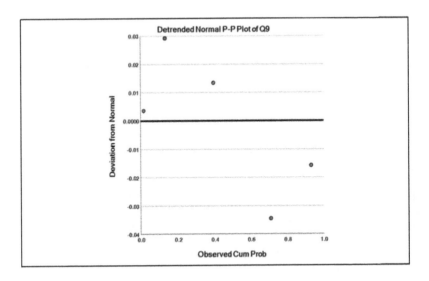

Q10

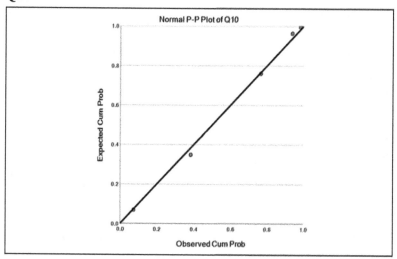

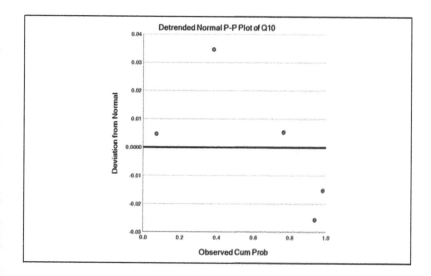

Q11

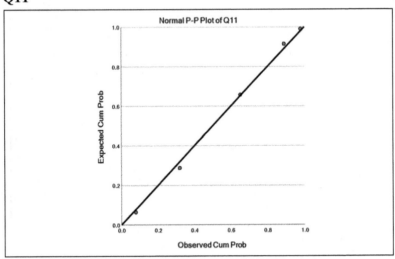

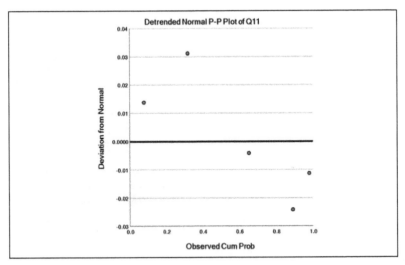

Appendix C6. P-P Plots.

Appendix D:
Chi-Square Test for Independence

Tested Pair	Person Chi-Square	df	Asymptotic Significance (2-sided)
Q1 & Q2*	36.475	16	0.002
Q1 & Q3*	30.4	16	0.016
Q1 & Q4	24.911	16	0.071
Q1 & Q5*	30.779	16	0.014
Q1 & Q6	21.894	16	0.147
Q1 & Q7	23.094	16	0.111
Q1 & Q8*	35.787	16	0.003
Q1 & Q9*	39.398	16	0.001
Q1 & Q10*	32.724	16	0.008
Q1 & Q11	25.024	16	0.069
Q2 & Q3*	43.26	16	0.000
Q2 & Q4*	37.92	16	0.002
Q2 & Q5	24.655	16	0.076
Q2 & Q6*	33.223	16	0.007
Q2 & Q7	24.449	16	0.080
Q2 & Q8*	30.699	16	0.015
Q2 & Q9	19.612	16	0.238
Q2 & Q10	21.716	16	0.153
Q2 & Q11*	29.806	16	0.019
Q3 & Q4*	43.08	16	0.000
Q3 & Q5*	91.788	16	0.000
Q3 & Q6*	53.078	16	0.000
Q3 & Q7*	56.963	16	0.000
Q3 & Q8	25.194	16	0.066
Q3 & Q9*	30.508	16	0.016
Q3 & Q10*	41.103	16	0.001
Q3 & Q11*	43.827	16	0.000
Q4 & Q5*	60.274	16	0.000
Q4 & Q6*	140.465	16	0.000
Q4 & Q7*	121.5	16	0.000
Q4 & Q8	23.485	16	0.101
Q4 & Q9	25.394	16	0.063
Q4 & Q10*	92.834	16	0.000
Q4 & Q11*	81.526	16	0.000

Q5 & Q6*	112.675	16	0.000
Q5 & Q7*	76.728	16	0.000
Q5 & Q8*	37.823	16	0.002
Q5 & Q9*	42.394	16	0.000
Q5 & Q10*	113.774	16	0.000
Q5 & Q11*	88.314	16	0.000
Q6 & Q7*	137.933	16	0.000
Q6 & Q8	23.663	16	0.097
Q6 & Q9*	27.689	16	0.034
Q6 & Q10*	157.395	16	0.000
Q6 & Q11*	120.479	16	0.000
Q7 & Q8*	47.803	16	0.000
Q7 & Q9*	39.345	16	0.001
Q7 & Q10*	146.548	16	0.000
Q7 & Q11*	102.332	16	0.000
Q8 & Q9*	249.657	16	0.000
Q8 & Q10*	28.355	16	0.029
Q8 & Q11*	38.729	16	0.001
Q9 & Q10*	34.749	16	0.004
Q9 & Q11*	43.825	16	0.000
Q10 & Q11*	128.063	16	0.000
*) significant at the 0.05 level			

Appendix D. Chi-Square Test for Independence.

About The Author

Dr. Faton Aliu
Owner and President, PECB

With over 25 years of professional experience spanning quality and information security management, project management, IT, consulting, training, and auditing, Faton has consistently demonstrated a system-oriented approach and exceptional leadership. His tenure at PECB has been marked by significant achievements, where he has been instrumental in driving corporate goals and strategies and overseeing the entire workforce. Faton's role involves providing inspirational leadership and direction to executives, fostering a culture of effective decision-making, and ensuring PECB's continued development toward achieving short- and long-term objectives.

Beyond his responsibilities at PECB, he serves on the Board of Directors of the International Personnel Certification Association (IPC) and contributes to Canadian committees/working groups for ISO/IEC 20000 and ISO/IEC 38500. His professional journey includes serving as the CEO of DCE Group, specializing in ISO standards implementation, and as the Educational Technologies Director at the American University in Kosova.

Faton holds a doctorate from École des Ponts Business School in Paris, a master's degree in service management from the Rochester Institute of Technology, and executive certificates in Mergers and Acquisitions, Cybersecurity, and Open Innovation from Harvard University. Additionally, he holds certifications, including ISO/IEC 27001 Master, Quality Systems Manager, ISO 9001 Lead Auditor, ISO/IEC 20000 Implementer, ISO/IEC 27001 Lead Auditor, ISO/IEC 27001 Lead Implementer, and CE Marking Counselor. Faton is passionate about leveraging his expertise and experience to drive meaningful impact and growth in PECB and the broader professional community.

Contact the author:
faton.aliu@pecb.com
https://www.linkedin.com/in/fatonaliu/

About PECB

PECB is a leading certification body dedicated to fostering digital trust through comprehensive education, certification, and certificate programs across various disciplines. We empower professionals to develop and demonstrate their competence in digital security and other areas of expertise by providing world-class certification programs that adhere to internationally recognized standards.

Why Choose PECB?
At PECB, we are committed to your success. We work closely with you to understand your unique challenges and provide tailored training solutions that meet your specific needs. Our goal is to help you build a secure digital future, protect your business integrity, and ensure operational resilience.

Expertise and Accreditation:
At PECB, we blend deep expertise with globally recognized and accredited training portfolio. Our training courses are designed by industry leaders and adhere to the highest standards.

Flexible Learning Options:
We offer flexible learning options, allowing you to access our training programs online or in-person, so you can learn at your own pace.

Industry-Relevant Training:
Our training programs are continuously updated to reflect the latest industry trends and threats. This ensures that you receive the most current and relevant information to protect your organization effectively.

Global Reach:
Our extensive network of over 2,600 partners and 2,100 trainers globally, ensuring you receive top-tier training and support, no matter where you are located, providing you with consistent quality and accessibility.

PECB's Comprehensive Portfolio
We offer diverse education solutions designed to meet the demands of various industries and roles, ensuring Digital Trust.

The primary services are grouped as follows:
1. **Professional Courses:** Choose from over 300 tailored training courses to meet diverse industry needs and career levels. Whether you are just starting or seeking to advance your expertise, our diverse portfolio offers training courses designed to meet your goals.

2. **Cybersecurity Technical Courses:** Delve into in-depth security courses with technical know-how and hands-on labs in a simulated environment that will prepare you for real-life challenges.

3. **PECB Skills:** Unlock a world of knowledge with expert-led video capsules and certificate programs, with select courses accredited by ANAB. These are perfect for continuous learning at your convenience!

4. **PECB Connect:** Take your auditing career to the next level by becoming a world-renowned Management System Auditor and joining the platform that serves as a bridge between certification bodies and auditors.

For more information, contact PECB at:
support@pecb.com
+1-844-426-7322
6683 Jean Talon E, Suite 336, Montreal, H1S 0A5, QC, Canada, or reach out directly through our website **www.pecb.com**.

We're here to support you every step of the way!